OFFICE PROOFREADING

Janet Pigott B Ed (Hons)
Senior Lecturer
Department of Secretarial and Commercial Studies
Walsall College of Technology

Marion Smith
Fellow of the Royal Society of Arts

STANLEY THORNES (PUBLISHERS) LIMITED

© Janet Pigott and Marion Smith 1986

All rights reserved. No part of this publication may be reproduced, stored in a retrieval system or transmitted in any form or by any means, electronic, mechanical, photocopying, recording or otherwise, without prior written consent of the copyright holders. Applications for such permission should be addressed to the publishers: Stanley Thornes (Publishers) Ltd, Old Station Drive, Leckhampton, Cheltenham GL53 0DN, Gloucestershire.

First published in 1986 by
Stanley Thornes (Publishers) Ltd
Old Station Drive
Leckhampton
Cheltenham GL53 0DN

British Library Cataloguing in Publication Data

Pigott, Janet
   Office proofreading.
   1. Commercial correspondence   2. Proof-reading
   I. Title   II. Smith, Marion
   808'.066651021   HF5726

ISBN 0-85950-550-2

Typeset in 11/13 Cheltenham Light by Rondale Design, Lydney, Gloucestershire.
Printed and bound in Great Britain at The Bath Press, Avon.

Contents

Acknowledgements   1

Aims   2

1 Proofreading explained   3
    1.1 Spot the differences   3
    1.2 Noticing mistakes   4
    1.3 Technical terms   5
    1.4 Basic terminology   5
    1.5 House rules and house style   6
    1.6 Questions   6

2 Searching for errors   8
    2.1 Working individually   8
    2.2 Dictating on tape   11
    2.3 Working in pairs   11
    2.4 Questions   11

3 Types of errors   12
    3.1 Keyboarding errors   12
    3.2 Spelling errors   13
    3.3 Word omitted   15
    3.4 Line(s) omitted   16
    3.5 Word or syllable repeated
        or left out   17
    3.6 Figures (numerals)   18
    3.7 Punctuation   23
    3.8 Word substitution   25
    3.9 Audio mistranscription   26
    3.10 Grammar   27
    3.11 Capitalisation   28
    3.12 Homophones   28
    3.13 Spacing   30
    3.14 Hyphenation   31
    3.15 Handwriting   32
    3.16 Shorthand   34
    3.17 Questions   35

4 Screenreading   36
    4.1 Status (formatting) line   36
    4.2 Ruler line   37
    4.3 Control flags and
        screen symbols   39

4.4	Word wraparound	39
4.5	Hard spaces	41
4.6	Soft spaces	43
4.7	Protected spaces	43
4.8	Reformed text	45
4.9	Toggle action commands	48
4.10	Forgotten commands	49
4.11	Misinterpretation errors	53
4.12	Questions	56
4.13	Glossary	57

5 Proof correction symbols — 60
    5.1 Proof correction symbols 60
    5.2 Questions 63

6 Practical proofreading exercises — 64

7 Key to questions and exercises — 110

8 External examination questions — 116

Index — 123

Acknowledgements

The authors would like to thank the following for their kind permission to reproduce material in this publication:

The British Standards Institution, for printer's proof correction symbols listed in BS 5261;

The London Chamber of Commerce and Industry Examinations Board, for past examination questions;

The Royal Society of Arts Examinations Board, for past examination questions.

Faber and Faber Ltd are thanked for their kind permission to base a proof-reading exercise on, and quote from, the poem 'The Whitsun Weddings' by the late Dr Philip Larkin, published in the book *The Whitsun Weddings* (Faber and Faber, 1964).

Mrs Margaret Rees-Boughton is thanked for reading through the script and offering advice, and the help given by Frank Farrell, Karynne, Nigel and Peter Pigott is gratefully acknowledged.

Janet Pigott
Marion Smith

Aims

The aim of this book is to help typists, word processor operators, pupils in commercial streams, secretarial students in colleges, and trainee text processor operators on YTS, 17+, 25+, TVEI, CPVE and similar schemes to detect errors quickly on hard copy and on soft copy on a visual display unit, and to give practice in how to react to those errors.

Although this book should be useful for anyone studying for practical typewriting and word processing examinations (such as RSA, LCCI, JEB, Pitman, West Midlands Examinations Board, GCSE, etc) as well as preparing the secretary already in employment to become more aware of the various kinds of errors which can slip by unnoticed, it is not intended to be a typing book; nor is it intended for use by typists only. Its prime aim is to be a reading-and-correcting book which will be of benefit to everyone in schools and colleges, at work or at home, to become skilled in proof-reading and proof correction techniques.

Ways of using the book

Scan the entire book quickly for
pleasure and initial assessment. *(student and teacher)*

Read each section individually then
answer the end-of-section questions. *(student)*

Check the end-of-section questions with
the answers in the key (chapter 7). *(student)*

Re-read all the examples and exercises,
reaching your own conclusions about the errors.
This could be a **discussion** activity. *(student and teacher)*

Work through the examples, carefully
tracing across as indicated in section 2.
Make notes of the differences between the
originals and drafts. *(student)*

Discuss the methods of marking up the
errors with a colleague, teacher or
fellow student. *(student and teacher)*

Correct the errors in pencil, but only if the book
is your personal property. College or school copies
should not be marked. *(student)*

Type out correct versions and carry
out further proofreading of the newly
typed script against the original. *(student)*

1 Proofreading explained

Proofreading means looking, comparing, and searching for uniformities and dissimilarities between two versions of an item. It can be thought of as a 'spot the differences' game. Start by looking at the drawings below.

1.1 Spot the differences

How many differences can you see between the picture on the right and the picture on the left?

If you were told that there were fifteen differences, would you be satisfied once you had found that number?

If you didn't know how many differences there were, would you give up looking after you had found the most obvious ones?

By finding the differences, you have 'proofread' the drawings: that is, you have looked at the original and the draft, compared them, found similarities and differences, and *noted* the differences.

1.2 Noticing mistakes

Now imagine yourself seeing the following five notices – in a shop, in a shop window, on a notice board, on a gatepost, in a gateway. Even without comparing them with what their authors originally had in mind, you can doubtless spot the errors.

NO PARKING HERE – DOTORS'S ENTERANCE

**POLITE NOTICE
NO PARKIING**

PROPERTY AQUIRED BY KING & Co FOR OFFICE EXTENTION

FOR SAIL £100 DEPPOSIT

TOMATOS 12p. PER ¼ lb

Looking for differences in pictures is fun. We enjoy spotting the changes, especially if the task is competitive, and there is the possibility of a prize at the end of it. But looking for differences in written and printed work is much more difficult, and we never know in advance how many differences there are going to be. Therefore we have to be trained in *how* to look – and what to look for – and what to do about the differences once we have found them.

In the office, the 'spot the differences' process is concerned mainly with words and layouts. The quest to detect errors in typed and printed work is called proofreading, and the person who does the searching is called a proofreader.

1.3 Technical terms

In the production of a copy of a document, there are several different terms in use. A *photocopy* provides a facsimile reproduction – an exact copy in every detail, usually in black and white. A typist-secretary produces a *faircopy* which means a clear, clean, pleasing-to-the-eye typed reproduction or transcription with all the corrections done. A word-processing secretary would input the information required, which goes at first into the computer's internal memory, and on many operating systems a *softcopy* can be read at the same time on a television-type screen called a visual display unit or VDU. Some non-display word processors commit the keyed-in text to magnetic tape attached to (or inside) the hardware. But whether the text can be read on screen or not, the final copy is printed out, either on a separate printer or on the non-display word processor itself. This final copy is referred to as a *hardcopy* or a *printout*.

The term 'proof' comes from the printing industry, and means the first printed impression taken for checking and correcting.

The 'context' is the general meaning of an extract.

1.4 Basic terminology

Basic terminology used throughout this book:

(a) *Original* – the first version provided by the author. It may be manuscript, typescript, amended print, dictation or a mixture of them all.

(b) *Draft* – the typed/printed version (made from the original) that has to be checked.

(c) *Final version* – the corrected draft.

All typed and printed work, softcopies and hardcopies, must be checked to detect and correct errors which have occurred. A professional proofreader in the printing industry must never trust that even the original (or rough draft) will be accurate; rather the opposite. The proofreader may experience a sense of achievement when errors are found. The typist, keyboard operator or secretary may find it annoying to discover mistakes which have to be corrected before multiple copies of the final version can safely be produced.

There will be many different types of errors – not just typographic ones (typing or keyboarding mistakes). There may be spelling mistakes, wrong division of words at line endings, words omitted or inserted, wrong spacing after punctuation marks, characters such as brackets, quotation marks and so on inserted at the beginning or end of a section and not at the other, incorrect line spacing, transposed characters or words, grammatical mistakes, wrong homophones (same-sounding words like tire/tyre) used, and so on.

1.5 House rules and house style

Another important aspect for the proofreader to check is that the display of the work is in keeping with the company's house style and that any house rules about spellings, capitalisation, hyphenation and layout have been followed. For example, a house rule may allow alternative spellings such as 'disk' and 'disc', 'recognise' and 'recognize', 'moneys' and 'monies', 'instal' and 'install'. The spelling should be consistent throughout the document and alternative spellings should not appear in different parts of it.

House rules could state also that compound words should not be hyphenated: 'proofread' for 'proof-read', 'microcomputer' for 'micro-computer', 'hardcopy' for 'hard-copy', 'filmstrip' for 'film-strip' and so on. House rules may apply also to the use of fractions and symbols, for example '10%' or 'ten per cent', '5¼' or '5.25' etc.

House style will be based on custom and practice within the company. A traditional office, no matter how busy, may prefer letters to be displayed in *semi-blocked* style (with centred headings, indented paragraphs and the signature block commencing half-way across the page); or an *indented style* (where each line in the company's address, addressee, and complimentary close are indented five spaces to the right).

Another company may prefer a *fully-blocked* style of letter (where every line begins at the same scale point on the left), with or without 'open' punctuation (no full-stops, commas or other punctuation marks in the reference, date, addressee, salutation or complimentary close). Whenever a proofreader is in doubt, the house rules should be referred to. Doubtful spellings should always be checked in a standard English dictionary.

1.6 Questions

1. A photocopy provides a f_____ which means that the original has been reproduced in exact detail, except c_____.

2. A fair copy is a neatly typed version of an original, and in this book is referred to as a d_____ which has to be c_____.

3. When all the mistakes have been located and corrected, the acceptable copy is referred to as the f_____ v_____.

4. The printed-out version of text which has been produced on a word processor's printer is called a h_____ p_____.

5   The first impression taken by a printer for checking and correction is called a p_____.

6   The person who inspects, checks and corrects the first printed impression is called a p_____.

7   To be consistent throughout, a set of h_____ r_____ and the h_____ s_____ should be adhered to.

Searching for errors

Because people read what they think they see, rather than what they actually see, they must be trained to read every word individually – and sometimes letter by letter. Do not skim through the work, or read groups of words quickly (as if reading for pleasure), because mistakes can be easily missed. As soon as a mistake is detected it should be marked immediately using, preferably, the appropriate printer's proof correction symbols in the margin and the text body. If the mistake is not marked up immediately, it may be forgotten; if not forgotten, it may take a long time to find again.

In elementary office proofreading it may be sufficient to circle the errors as they are found. Some people use their own methods of indicating alterations, amendments and corrections. A list of selected signs and symbols is given in Chapter 5. These are the ones to use in all the practice proofreading exercises.

In the printing industry, compositors (typesetters) will disregard anything marked on the proofs in pencil, so it is good working practice to use the correct technique in the office. A ball-point, felt-tip, or fountain pen should be used.

There are three basic methods of searching for errors:

2.1 Working individually

A proofreader can work individually. The draft should always be checked against the original, and the two versions should be placed side by side. The reader should imagine a line down the centre of the draft.

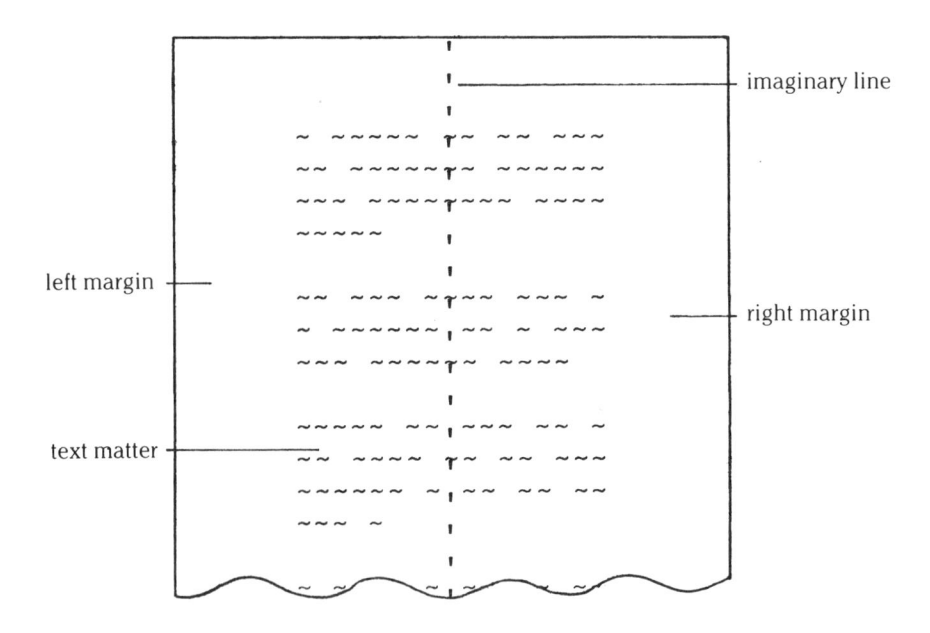

The words are traced individually by a finger along each line of the draft, and followed at the same time on the original. As soon as a mistake is found, it should be marked with the right symbol in text and margin. Marginal correction symbols should be placed on the same horizontal line as the mistake. If the mistake falls in the left half of the page, the symbol should be written in the left margin.

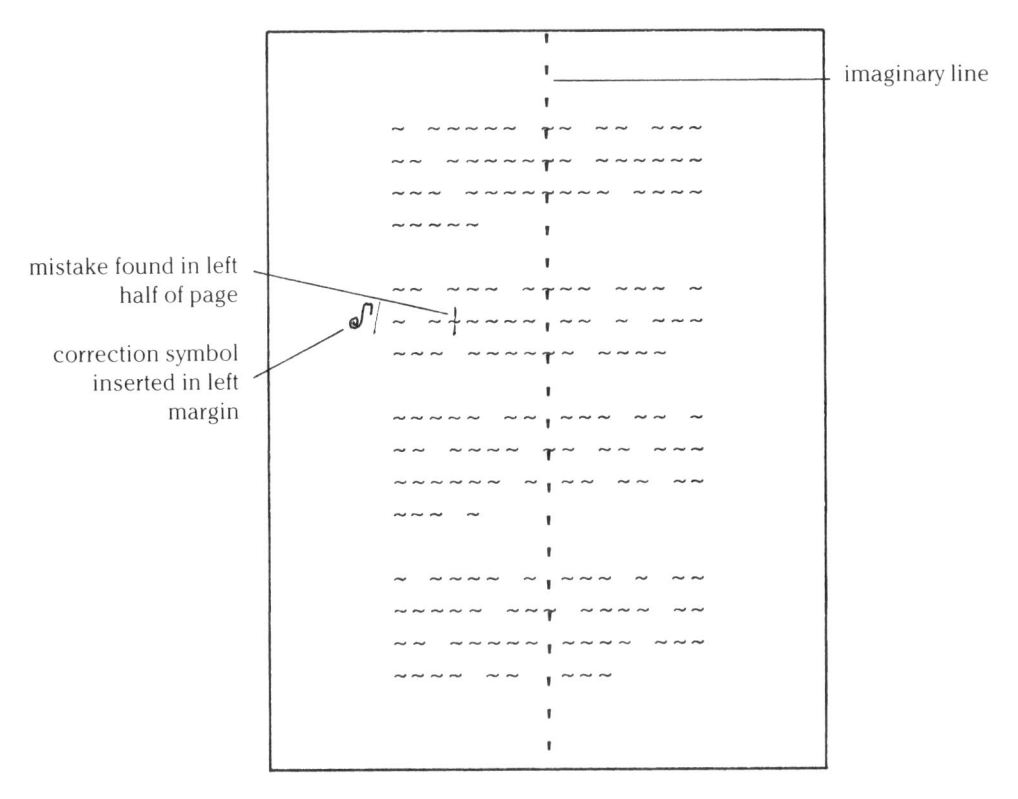

[Diagram showing a page with an imaginary vertical line down the center. A mistake found in the left half of the page has a correction symbol inserted in the left margin on the same horizontal line.]

The correction symbol should be placed close to the text so that if a second mistake is found on the same horizontal line, but still in the left half of the page, a second symbol can be placed in the left margin, working outwards from the text:

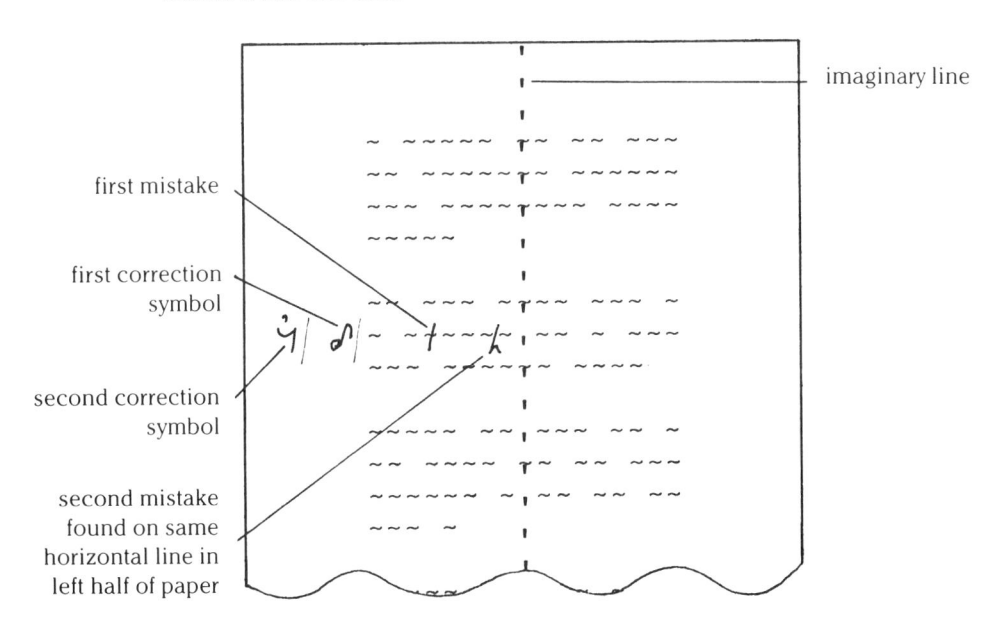

[Diagram showing a page with an imaginary vertical line down the center. A first mistake and a second mistake on the same horizontal line in the left half of the paper have their correction symbols placed in the left margin, with the second correction symbol placed outwards from the first.]

Errors in the right half of the page are marked in the text and the correction symbol inserted in the right margin, working outwards from the text.

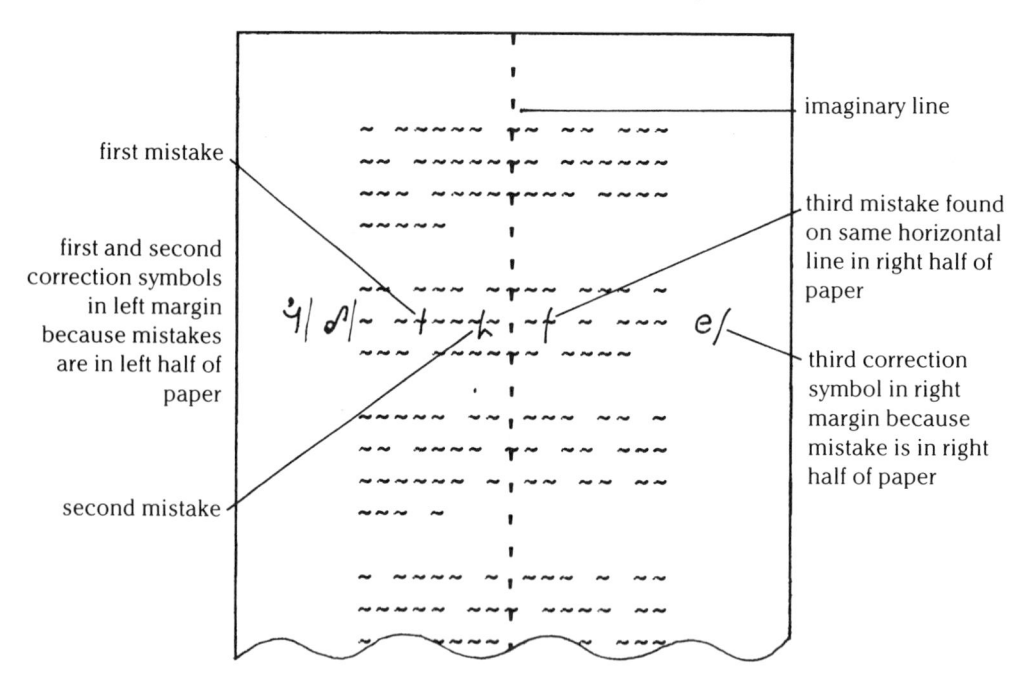

first mistake

first and second correction symbols in left margin because mistakes are in left half of paper

imaginary line

third mistake found on same horizontal line in right half of paper

third correction symbol in right margin because mistake is in right half of paper

second mistake

If a whole word (or a number of words) has to be inserted into the text and there is insufficient space in the appropriate margin, the opposite (and even the bottom) margins may be used. Handwritten amendments must always be clearly legible and should not be made sideways in a margin. In this case, work-flow is interrupted because the page usually has to be turned before it can be read.

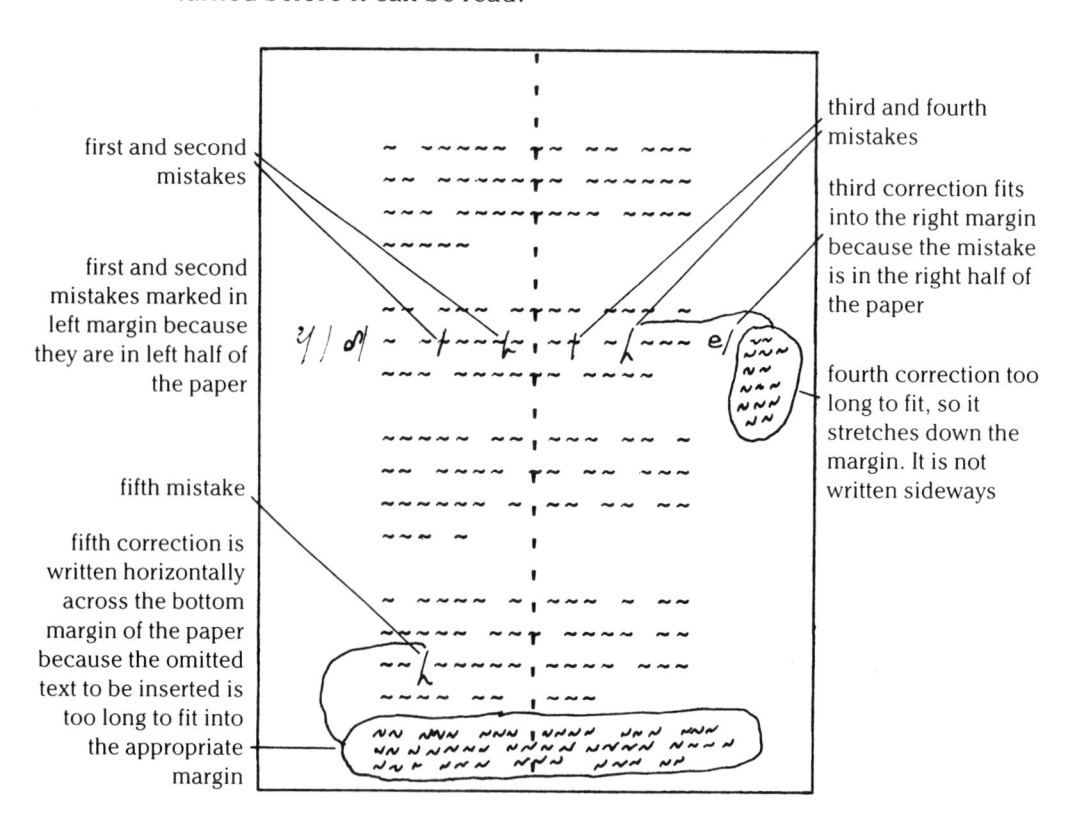

first and second mistakes

first and second mistakes marked in left margin because they are in left half of the paper

fifth mistake

fifth correction is written horizontally across the bottom margin of the paper because the omitted text to be inserted is too long to fit into the appropriate margin

third and fourth mistakes

third correction fits into the right margin because the mistake is in the right half of the paper

fourth correction too long to fit, so it stretches down the margin. It is not written sideways

2.2 Dictating on tape

A second method of checking, when working alone, is to dictate the text on an audio machine. When a mistake is found, the tape can be stopped while the error is marked up. This technique is useful because the tape can be played back many times over, and a headset and footpedal will ensure that the proofreader works quietly without interrupting anyone working nearby.

2.3 Working in pairs

The third method, widely used in large business offices, is to work with a colleague. One person (the caller) reads the original aloud and the other person (the proofreader) examines the draft, searching for errors and inserting correction symbols when mistakes are found. This method is much quicker than working alone, but the caller must have fluent reading ability in order to read accurately and clearly without hesitating or stumbling.

The caller's pronunciation must be clear enough to avoid confusion between Ps and Bs, Ts and Ds, and other similar sounds. The most important aspect of working together is that the pair should be a team, checking in unison, stopping to mark up the draft and taking a rest at appropriate page breaks. In lengthy work, it is wise to change activities from time to time, so that the proofreader becomes the caller, thus giving each other a break. The caller will need to read out punctuation marks, initial capitals, block capitals, headings, underscoring, word underscoring and so on. Technical names, place names, trade names and unusual names may have to be spelled out.

2.4 Questions

1 When checking a draft, the text should be read carefully w_____ by w_____.

2 Mistakes found should be marked up i_____ so that they are not forgotten or lost.

3 Correction symbols should be placed in the m_____ working o_____ from the text.

4 When checking for errors, the proofreader should check the d_____ against the o_____.

5 Because pencil marks are disregarded by professional printers, it is a good habit for the proofreader to mark the d_____ with any kind of p_____.

6 When corrections are too long to fit the appropriate margin, the b_____ margin may be used.

Types of errors

The secretary needs a good command of the language being used, an ability to use dictionaries and appropriate reference books, and knowledge of the types of error that may be encountered.

In proofreading, it is always assumed that the original version is available to proofread from. It will be found, however, that certain types of error are detectable without sight of the original. There may be occasions when the accuracy of the original is suspect: in these cases the proofreader needs to consult a dictionary and/or check with the author.

In this section, types of error have been classified and examples given of each. There are overlaps: for instance, an omitted letter might be simply a keyboarding error, or it may be caused by the proofreader's ignorance of a correct spelling. A substituted word might be caused by inaccurate copying, or by a keyboarding error.

3.1 Keyboarding errors

Errors which do not necessarily indicate weakness of language knowledge can be typographic. Such mistakes are made by striking the wrong key. Over-fast typing may produce:

Transposed letters	(*commenst* for *comments*)
A letter adjacent to the correct one	(*documemt* for *document*)
A right-finger-but-wrong-hand letter	(*setter* for *letter*)
or:	
A right-finger-but-wrong-row letter	(*wines* for *winds*)
A space omitted	(*thankyou* for *thank you*)
A letter omitted	(*secretry* for *secretary*)

Example 1 Eight keyboarding errors

Original

Draft

Original	Draft
When our ancestors came to this country they expected to find a land of milk and honey. Instead they were greeted by a cold blustery winter. Those who had quilts were thankful. These quilts were used not only as bedcovers but as rugs and wall hangings.	When our ancestors came to this country they expected to find a lamd of milk and honey. Insetad they were gretted by a cold blustery ointer. Those who had quilts were thandful. These quits were used not only as bedcobers but as rugs and wallhangings.

Example 2 One keyboarding error

Original	Draft
It is possible that other problems would be encountered in schools which use more than one major scheme, or which use a "box" system.	It is possible that other problems would be encounted in schools which use more than one major scheme, or which use a "box" system.

Example 3 Two keyboarding errors

Original	Draft
Turn off the electricity before papering around sockets and light switches.	Turn off the electricty before papering round sockets and light switches.

Example 4 One keyboarding error in each sentence

Original	Draft
He wrote to say that he would be willing to act as a proxy voter at the poll.	(a) He wrote to say that he would be willing to act as a proxy voter at the pool.
She tried very hard to win in the Obstacle Race.	(b) She tried very hard to sin in the Obstacle Race.
The letter from Kate was beautifully written.	(c) The letter from Date was beautifully written.
We crossed the Channel safely in our yacht.	(d) We crossed the Channel safely in our yatch.

3.2 Spelling errors

If the original is being read out to a proofreader, the caller should spell out 'tricky' words which could be wrong in the draft. The proofreader also needs to be on the lookout for these and others: there may be an error in the original, in which case the proofreader must consult a dictionary, and/or check with the author.

(a) Common errors Full lists cannot be given here, but the following selection indicates the sort of error which is commonly made.

accoustic	harrassed	
benefitted	occassionally/ocassionally	
concensus	oportunity	
consummable	proceedures	
contracters	proffesional/proffessional	*(Every word*
definate	seperate	*in the list is*
embarassed	supercede	*incorrect.)*

(b) Spellings dependent on parts of speech Particular care is necessary with similar pairs of words.

practice – practise	(noun – verb)
advice – advise	(noun – verb)
dependant – dependent	(noun – adjective)

The *meaning* of the passage is important here: the proficient typist should be capable of deciding whether the right word has been used.

Example 5 Three incorrect spellings

```
My advise was that we should discontinue the prac-
tice of notifying dependents so far in advance,
because often we had to repeat the notification
later.  We needed to practice economy in postage,
so we advised the officers accordingly.
```

(c) Inconsistent spelling A word is sometimes correct in one part of a paragraph but misspelled in another.

Example 6

```
In the circumstances of this case, and given the
level of competence expected, I do not think it
was negligent not to make this diagnosis.  In
retrospect there are some aspects of the case
that might have been handled differently, but the
actions taken do not amount to negligance in my
opinion.
```

(d) Confusion of ... ie ... and ... ei ... English has more exceptions than rules, and the relationship between sound and spelling has to be memorised.

Sound of EE	(ie)	as in *believe*
Sound of EE	(ei)	as in *seize*
Sound of EE	(ei after c)	as in *receive*
Sound of AY	(ei)	as in *weight*
Sound of EYE	(ei)	as in *height*
Exceptions	(ei)	as in *leisure*

(There are occasional ambiguities: a word like *neither* may be pronounced as 'n-eye-ther' or 'n-ee-ther'.)

Example 7

The words listed here can be arranged in six groups, as indicated by the table:

achieve	ceiling	relief	seize	chief
receipt	being	belief	beige	deity
siesta	sieve	fiend	friend	reign
diesel	either	neither	Einstein	eight
field	perceive	conceited	counterfeit	

Sound:

EE (ie)	EE (ei)	EE (ei after c)	AY (ei)	EYE (ei)	Exception
7 words	2 or 4 words	4 words	3 words	1 or 3 words	5 or 6 words

(Please do not write on page.)

3.3 Word omitted

Omission of a word may give the opposite meaning to the one intended.

Example 8

Original	Draft
Allowing a child to skip certain sections of a reader is based on the belief that it is not necessary to read every word of every page.	Allowing a child to skip certain sections of a reader is based on the belief that it is necessary to read every word of every page.

Omission of a word may still make sense, without reference to the original.

Example 9

Original	Draft
The Olympic gymnast from the USA won three gold medals.	The gymnast from USA won three gold medals.

In other cases, omission of a word will not make sense.

Example 10

Original	Draft
The Lord Mayor will be opening the new Zoo next Saturday.	The Lord Mayor will be the new Zoo next Saturday.

3.4 Line(s) omitted

This type of error will be discovered easily if the original is read aloud to the proofreader. If it is not read aloud, the passage may appear to make sense. In the next example, the typist has jumped from the first 'measure' to the second.

Example 11

Original	Draft
To find out how many rolls to buy, first measure the height of the walls from skirting to ceiling, and measure the distance around the entire room, including doors and windows.	To find out how many rolls to buy, first measure the distance around the entire room, including doors and windows.

Omission of a line makes nonsense of the following passage.

Example 12

Original	Draft
Two important managerial problems which rapidly became apparent were a lack of money for equipment, and a lack of training for staff.	Two managerial problems which rapidly became apparent were a lack of training for staff.

3.5 Word or syllable repeated or left out

People usually read what they think they see.

Example 13

```
TRAVEL AND
AND HOLIDAY PLANNING
```

```
Top of
the
the bill
```

A word or syllable may be repeated or omitted at a line end.

Example 14

> The undersigned end-user of
> XYZ software hereby acknow-
> knowledges that he or she
> has read, and fully under-
> stands, the terms of the
> end-user agreement.

> The undersigned end-user
> of XYZ software hereby ack-
> ledges that he or she has
> read, and fully understands,
> the terms of the end-user
> agreement.

3.6 Figures (numerals)

(a) Keyboarding errors   These will often not be apparent unless the original is read aloud to the proofreader.

Example 15

Original	Draft
Daily units used: 1.155, 3.429, 1,109, 10,000, 2,051, 1,760	Daily units used: 1.115, 3.429, 1,009, 10,000, 2,050, 1,760

If a set of numbers shows a pattern (for example, of increase or decrease) an error is easier to spot.

Example 16

Original	Draft
Recommended price: £25, £30, £31, £41, £43, £53, £62.	Recommended price: £25, £30, £31, £41, £34, £53, £62

(b) *Impossible figures* can usually be discovered even without the aid of the original.

Example 17

```
on 31 April 1986 ...

... hydrotherapy baths kept at a temperature of 98 °C ...

It is suggested that the dose be increased from 200 mg
daily to 150 mg daily.
```

(c) *Figures that can be checked easily* In this case, either the total is wrong or one of the items is wrong.

Example 18

£60
£15
£12
£35
£112

(d) Consistency of 1 *and* 0   Some typewriters have a figure (numeral) one (1) and a lower-case el (l). Some typewriters have a nought (0) and an upper-case letter O.

These should not be mixed in any one piece of work. Example 19 shows incorrect use.

Example 19

```
21 May - 31 July
20 May - 30 June
```

It should read:

```
21 May - 31 July    or    21 May - 31 July
20 May - 30 June    or    20 May - 30 June
```

Computers are not programmed to calculate letters of the alphabet, so for calculations the figures 1 and 0 must be used.

(e) Roman numerals   Points to check particularly are: that upper-case letters and lower-case letters are used consistently:

   I V X L C D M   or   i v x l c d m.

Example 20

```
Grade lll (Advanced)
```
This is incorrect (it reads 'one hundred and eleven').

It should read like this.

```
Grade III (Advanced)
```

Example 21

This is wrong.

> XX1V

This, with upper-case I in place of 1, is correct.

> XXIV

Example 22

Here the typist needs to know whether all Arabic figures, or all Roman numerals, are required.

```
The degrees of difficulties have been graded.
Grade 1 is the easiest; Grades II and III are
progressively more difficult; and Grade 4 is
the most difficult.
```

Example 23

Alignment must be accurate.

This is wrong.

```
Section    X
          XII
         XIII
          XIV
```

If the numbers are correctly copied, it should be typed like this.

```
Section    X
         XII
        XIII
         XIV
```

If the numbers were incorrectly copied, and were intended to form a sequence, it should be typed like this.

```
Section   XI
         XII
        XIII
         XIV
```

(f) Postcodes need careful checking. A postcode has two halves, separated by a space.

Example 24

This is wrong.

```
M502AG
```

The second half of the postcode always begins with a single figure.

Example 25

This is incorrect. It is more likely to be 1AG; that is, with a figure one instead of a capital I.

```
M50 IAG
```

Example 26

This is likely to have been miscopied from B67 1BG.

```
B67 I8G
```

Example 27

This is likely to be B67 5AG.

```
B67 SAG
```

(g) Telephone numbers   Look out for impossible numbers.

Example 28

```
(Birmingham)    021-558 3232
(Glasgow)       041-221 2581
(Liverpool)     951-236 8464
(Manchester)    061-236 9456
```

All STD (subscriber trunk dialling) codes begin with 0. The Liverpool code above is incorrect.

(h) Dates   Check dates rigorously in important documents.

Example 29

```
CONFERENCE DATES IN 1986

6 - 8  January   Edinburgh
8 -10  May       London
2 - 4  July      Bristol
```

The first two items are Thursday to Saturday; the third is Wednesday to Friday. This would need checking.

3.7 Punctuation

Look out for incomplete 'pairs': brackets, commas, quotation marks, dashes.

Example 30

Original	Draft
Moira said, "Not many people are good divers, are they?" The attendant said, "No. But most people (thank goodness) are capable swimmers."	Moira said, "Not many people are good divers, are they? The attendant said, "No. But most people (thank goodness are capable swimmers.
Electrostatic copiers produce, very quickly, as many or as few copies as required.	Electrostatic copiers produce, very quickly as many or as few copies as required.
The chairman – the new one – presided at both meetings.	The chairman – the new one, presided at both meetings.
These Councils were at their most active between 1959 and 1967, when they reported on 15-18 provision (Crowther), education 13-16 (Newsom), and lastly, "primary education in all its aspects" (Plowden).	These Councils were at their most active between 1959 and 1967, when they reported on 15-18 provision (Crowther), education 13-16 (Newsom, and lastly, "primary education in all its aspects (Plowden).

Punctuation left out may alter the intended meaning.

Example 31

Original	Draft
If "reading" to a particular teacher means "word recognition", she will drill on basic sight vocabulary and word-recognition skills.	If reading to a particular teacher means word recognition, she will drill on basic sight vocabulary and word-recognition skills.

Look out for overlapping sentences: that is, misplacing a full stop so that the beginning of one sentence is attached to the end of the one before.

Example 32

Original	Draft
Metal plates can produce tens of thousands of copies. If only several hundred are needed, a paper plate is more economical.	Metal plates can produce tens of thousands of copies if only several hundred are needed. A paper plate is more economical.
Firms may change their names because of mergers or takeovers. People change their names, especially women, when they get married.	Firms may change their names. Because of mergers or takeovers, people change their names, especially women when they get married.
Lateral filing cabinets take up less floor space. As there are no drawers to be opened, the files are arranged side by side.	Lateral filing cabinets take up less floor space, as there are no drawers. To be opened, the files are arranged side by side.

3.8 Word substitution

A word which is correct on its own, but wrong in context, may creep in. This type of error is probably the most difficult to spot easily. It occurs usually when one letter of a word is incorrectly copied: *is* for *it*; *as* for *has*; *is* for *his*; *now* for *not*. The proofreader must listen carefully to what is being read out, and must also think of the general meaning of a sentence as a whole.

Example 33

Original	Draft
There was no sensory weakness or reflex disturbance in the left arm.	There was no sensory weakness of reflex disturbance in the left arm.
Bare plaster surfaces are porous, and need a coat of size to seal and provide a good base.	Bare plaster surfaces are porous, and need a coat or size to seal and provide a good base.
The study laid down three conditions: (a) no drill on baseline, (b) drill on words, (c) drill on error words.	The study laid down three conditions: (a) no drill or baseline, (b) drill on words, (c) drill on error words.
The Gala will commence at the Queen Baths in London at 2 pm on 18 July.	The Gala will commence as the Queen Baths in London at 2 pm on 18 July.
These figures are obtained by totalling the number of words read correctly and words read incorrectly from each segment.	These figures are obtained by totally the number of words read correctly and words read incorrectly from each segment.

Example continued on the next page.

Example 33 continued.

It is proposed to carry out this project through a series of four introductory workshop sessions followed by a series of back-up sessions.	It is proposed to carry out this project through a series of four introductory workshop sessions following by a series of back-up sessions.
When joining lengths of wallpaper, a seam roller is useful for pressing the edges of the paper against the wall.	When joining lengths of wallpaper, a steam roller is useful for pressing the edges of the paper against the wall.
Walls are rarely properly vertical, so use a plumb line to ensure that the first length hangs true.	Walls are rarely properly vertical, so use a plum line to ensure that the first length hangs true.
It is anticipated that if this initial training is thorough, then there should be a corresponding reduction in the amount of time the psychologist needs to allocate to teachers in terms of support.	It is anticipated that if this initial training is through, then there should be a corresponding reduction in the amount of time the psychologist needs to allocate to teachers in terms of support.

3.9 Audio mistranscription

Audio transcriptions may cause problems. Frequently, inadequate instructions are given, or the typist does not have the ability to interpret the instructions properly. If the dictator's enunciation is not absolutely clear, it may be misheard or misinterpreted.

If the quality of the dictation is imperfect, some errors are difficult to spot. If the author is not available, it is probably best to ask someone else to listen to the recording while the transcript is read. In some cases, the context will indicate which of two possible versions is the right one: in other cases, only the author can check. In the following examples, the original or draft could be reasonably selected in four cases but not in the other two.

Example 34

Original	Draft
We enclose two copies of the contract: one is for your attention.	We enclose two copies of the contract: one is for your retention.
The recording shows asymmetrical tracing.	The recording shows a symmetrical tracing.
The pain increased in severity and infrequency, so that it would occur two or three times a day.	The pain increased in severity and in frequency, so that it would occur two or three times a day.
This recording shows atypical conformation.	This recording shows a typical conformation.
He complained of an increase in stiffness during the week.	He complained of increasing stiffness during the week.
... on account of the recurrent episodes of loss of awareness, and sometimes complete unresponsiveness for as long as twenty minutes at a time.	... on account of the current episodes of loss of awareness, and sometimes complete unresponsiveness for as long as twenty minutes at a time.

3.10 Grammar

See that nouns and verbs agree and that tenses are consistent. The first sentence below is correct: the next two are not.

Example 35

A person who uses a typewriter is referred to as a typist.

The reason for box numbers are to prevent people calling at firms instead of writing.

An application form must be completed and returned to the firm as quickly as possible, with a brief covering letter which state that the completed form is enclosed.

3.11 Capitalisation

These errors will not be heard when the material is read to the proofreader, so careful visual attention must be paid.

Example 36

Original	Draft
A loudspeaking telephone has a loudspeaker incorporated into the normal telephone dialling arrangement.	A loudspeaking telephone has a Loudspeaker incorporated into the normal telephone dialling arrangement.
He was invited to attend a party at the Plough Inn last Saturday. He and his wife enjoyed the function immensely.	He was invited to attend a Party at the Plough Inn last Saturday. He and his wife enjoyed the Function immensely.
The Rt Hon Gerald Langton MP was invited to attend a function at the Plough Inn last Saturday. He and his wife enjoyed the function, and thought the Plough Inn was a suitable venue.	The Rt hon Gerald Langton MP was invited to attend a function at the Plough Inn last Saturday. He and his wife enjoyed the function, and thought the Plough inn was a suitable venue.

3.12 Homophones

Read the following words one after the other:

isle sea weather their mite bee sum discrete weigh two meat hour principle guessed won mourning.

They sound like this sentence:

I'll see whether there might be some discreet way to meet our principal guest one morning.

The words are homophones. That is, they sound the same even though they have different spellings and meanings. Some of the commonest homophone errors are there/their, its/it's, who's/whose, principle/principal.

The brief definitions on the next page should help you to select the correct words in the sentences which follow.

Example 37

there	(adverb)	– in that place
their	(adjective)	– belonging to them
its	(adjective)	– belonging to it
it's	(noun + verb)	– short for *it is*
who's	(pronoun + verb)	– short for *who is*
whose	(adjective)	– belonging to whom
principle	(noun)	– belief
principal	(adjective)	– the most important
the Principal	(proper noun)	– the most important person

1 Their/There was a large queue so he decided not to wait.
2 A cat will carry a kitten by the scruff of its/it's neck.
3 He wondered who's/whose it was.
4 She ought to have complained to the principle/Principal before.
5 All the passengers had to carry their/there own cases.
6 I shall not go if its/it's foggy.
7 Whose/Who's going to do the washing up?
8 He said it was one of his principals/principles never to gamble.

Near-homophones are words which look and sound similar but have different meanings.

Example 38

were/where		
were	(verb)	– past tense of *are*
where	(adverb)	– in which place
accept/except		
to accept	(verb)	– to receive
except	(preposition)	– but for; save for
affect/effect		
to affect	(verb)	– to make a difference to
effect	(noun)	– the result of an action
to effect	(verb)	– to bring about

1 He forgot were/where he had put them.
2 They were/where all found eventually.
3 He was not willing to accept/except the present.

4 He chose all except/accept the blue ones.
5 His reduced salary will affect/effect his choice of new car.
6 The local council will effect/affect the change next year.
7 The effect/affect of the change may be small.

There are a great many homophones and near-homophones in the English language. If proofreaders are in doubt, they must check meanings with a dictionary.

3.13 Spacing

Extra spaces, or spaces left out, may be caused by machine faults or because the use of spaces is inconsistent.

Example 39

```
Ilook   forward  to  hearingfrom  you  as  soon   as
possible.
```

```
The Chairman - the new one- presided at both
meetings.
```

Spacing after punctuation, within and between sentences, must be consistent. Example 40 is incorrectly displayed.

Example 40

```
Franking machines may be purchased or hired from
manufacturers. A licence to use the machine must
first be obtained from the Post Office:  there is
no charge for this.  The Post Office also sets a
meter on a franking machine in accordance with the
amount of money paid to them,and then seals the
meter.  Each time an envelope,postcard or label is
franked,  this meter deducts the amount used-it is
 a  "descending " meter, as the figures shown
decrease. There is a second meter which increases
or " ascends" with each franked impression  -  this
shows the amount of postage used.
```

Spacing used with figures must be consistent.

Example 41

Opening times:	10 - 7	Ribbons:	£15.00
	9.30-7		£15. 20
	9.30 - 5.30		£12.00
	10-5		£12. 20

Note
When a right-hand margin is 'justified' (when the lines of type are adjusted to equal length, as often done on a word processor screen), spaces between words may be irregular. The next chapter explains this.

3.14 Hyphenation

Hyphens are important to meaning. Here are some examples.

re-cover has a different meaning from *recover*

Co-op has a different meaning from *coop*

more experienced teachers is not necessarily the same as *more–experienced teachers*

Consistency is important. If 'photocopy' is one word in part of a document, it should not appear as 'photo-copy' in another.

Words must sometimes be divided at the end of a line. Where this happens, the pronunciation of the whole word should be apparent from the part before the hyphen. *Pot-hole, dom-estic, wood-land, dis-cussion* are acceptable; *the-rapist, photoc-opy, opera-tor, rear-range* are not.

All the errors in this example are obvious to a trained proofreader.

Example 42

The current weak-ness in the price of crude oil is ca-used by over-supply reaching the market at a ti-me when the demand is seasonally at its lowe-st point. However, the general demand is impr-oving, so as the year progresses the market sho-uld become firmer.

3.15 Handwriting

There are many different styles of handwriting. However, few people adhere strictly to one style. They mix styles, and adapt characters to suit their own temperaments and personalities by adding hooks, loops, curves and other decoration. For example:

E may appear as:

G may appear as:

H may appear as:

T may appear as:

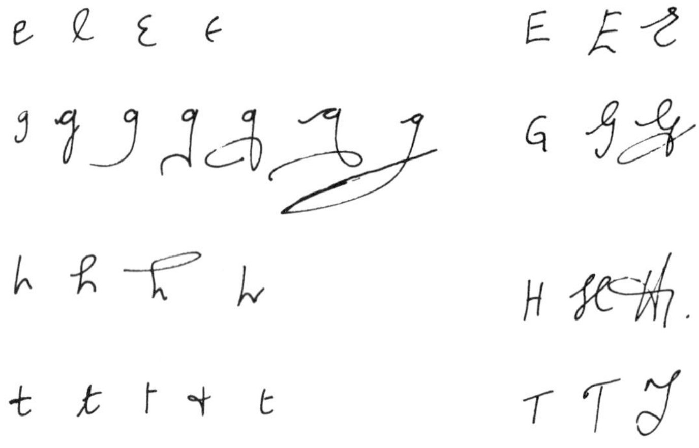

To interpret Example 43, it is necessary to study the handwriting carefully to discover how certain letters are made by this particular writer.

Example 43

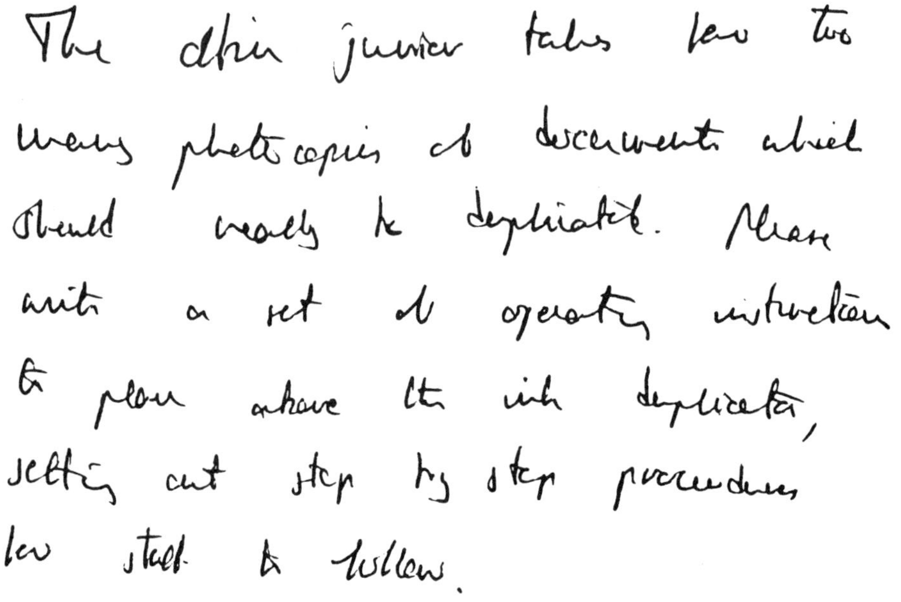

The office junior takes far too many photocopies of documents which should really be duplicated. Please write a set of operating instructions to place above the ink duplicator, setting out step by step procedures for staff to follow.

In some cases the original will be incorrect (there is a spelling error in Example 43). Amendments can be made before the draft is started.

Example 44

What do you think these sentences say?

Please order some new snibs for the windows.

The architect mailed her account for £3000.

Mr Bradshaw has an appointment for 9 am today

(Top) Some people would look at the fifth word several times. Is it *suils* or *snils* or *suits*, or any other word? It is in fact *snibs*. A snib is a small bolt or locking device for a window, and the sentence reads *Please order some new snibs for the windows*.

(Middle) The person referred to is the *architect* – not *auchitect* or *anchitect*. The real pitfall is in the fourth word: is the architect male or female? The sentence is intended to read *The architect mailed her account for £3000*. There is no dot over the middle letter of the fourth word; but the dots are there in words *architect* and *mailed*.

(Lower) This reads *Mr Bradshaw has an appointment for 9 am today*. The difficulty is in the time. The clue is the 'am': few offices are likely to be open at 7 am, so 9 am is more reasonable.

Signatures may be even more difficult to decipher: can these possibly be the signatures of G J Henderson, M Morrison and H Twigg? It is no use guessing. The proofreader needs to know in advance what the names are, or to have some version available in print or typescript.

Example 45

Handwritten numbers need equally careful scrutiny.

Example 46

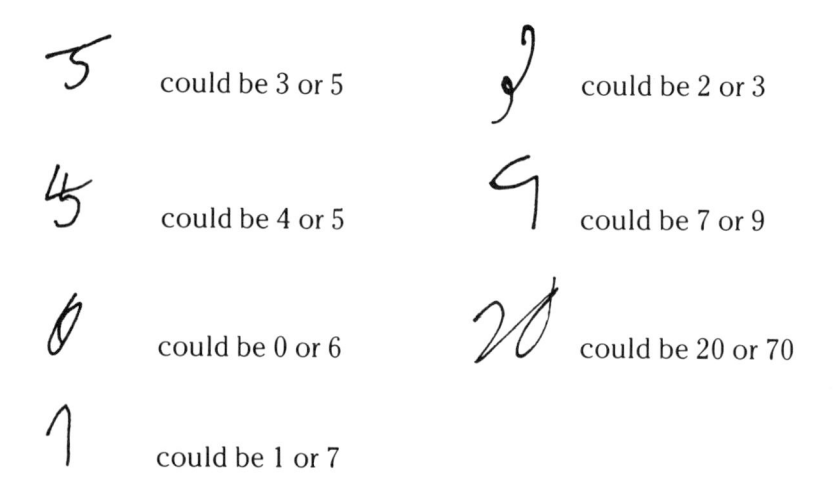

5 could be 3 or 5

2 could be 2 or 3

45 could be 4 or 5

9 could be 7 or 9

0 could be 0 or 6

20 could be 20 or 70

1 could be 1 or 7

The practice of writing *7* with one stroke through it, to distinguish it from *1*, is helpful.

3.16 Shorthand

Mistakes in the draft often arise from poor shorthand outlines. It is not possible to give examples from the many shorthand systems to illustrate such errors, but the reader could note whether those given below come from the system they use.

Example 47

Original dictation	*Draft transcription*
Thank you for your letter, which we have received through the hands of our assessors.	Thank you for your letter, which we have received from the handles of our saucepans.
Order No 7862 - 1 Blackboard and Easel	Order No 7862 - 1 Blackbird and Zulu
In analysing the contents of the packet we have tested the level of calcium.	In analysing the contents of the bag we have decided the lever is colossal.
This nugget appears to be available at 22 lb.	This antique appears to be valuable at £22.

Many transcription errors occur when short forms and phrases are misinterpreted. For example:

a		the
and the/to the		of the
as/has	*instead of*	is/his
with the		that the
for which		in which

3.17 Questions

1. The o_____ should always be available to proofread from, but certain types of errors are d_____ even without it.

2. Genuine typing errors could be:
   - (a) t_____ l_____
   - (b) a_____ k_____ struck
   - (c) right f_____ but wrong h_____ used
   - (d) faulty d_____ letters produced
   - (e) a s_____ or a letter omitted

3. Errors concerning the incorrect use of English could be:
   - (a) s_____ mistakes
   - (b) n_____ not agreeing with v_____
   - (c) wrong h_____ used
   - (d) incorrect p_____ used
   - (e) incorrect h_____ of words
   - (f) wrong c_____ used

4. The omission of a word, or line, may:
   - (a) give an o_____ meaning to that intended
   - (b) not make s_____ at all
   - (c) a_____ to be correct
   - (d) make n_____ of the passage

5. A word, or syllable, may have been r_____ or o_____ at a line-ending or line beginning.

6. Mistakes with figures are difficult to spot unless:
   - (a) the set p_____ does not conform
   - (b) they give i_____ information
   - (c) they can easily be c_____ by totalling.

Screenreading

All the points made so far in this book apply to screen reading, but there are additional technical features which have to be taken into account. People not familiar with the technical terms should refer to the glossary at the end of the chapter.

The purpose of a visual display unit is to display information stored in the computer's internal memory, or information which is accessed from an external storage medium such as a floppy or a hard disk. Most screens are capable of displaying twenty-two lines of text at a time; some display more, some less.

When reading a document on the screen, the first thing to check is the computer's information lines which are automatically displayed.

4.1 Status (formatting) line

This is the information line at the top of the screen. Every software manufacturer will have an individual style, and some may use a different name, but there will always be several common factors.

Here are examples of different styles of information lines.

Example 1 — **VDU**

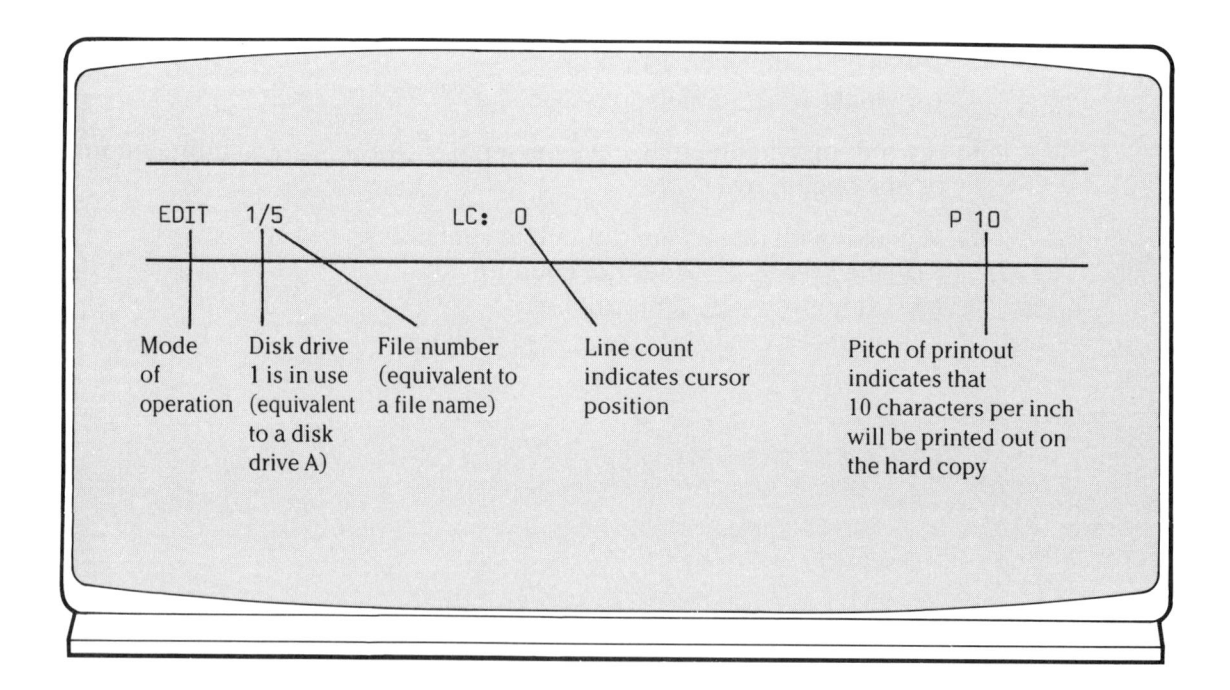

```
EDIT  1/5           LC:  0                              P 10
```

- Mode of operation
- Disk drive 1 is in use (equivalent to a disk drive A)
- File number (equivalent to a file name)
- Line count indicates cursor position
- Pitch of printout indicates that 10 characters per inch will be printed out on the hard copy

Example 2 — VDU

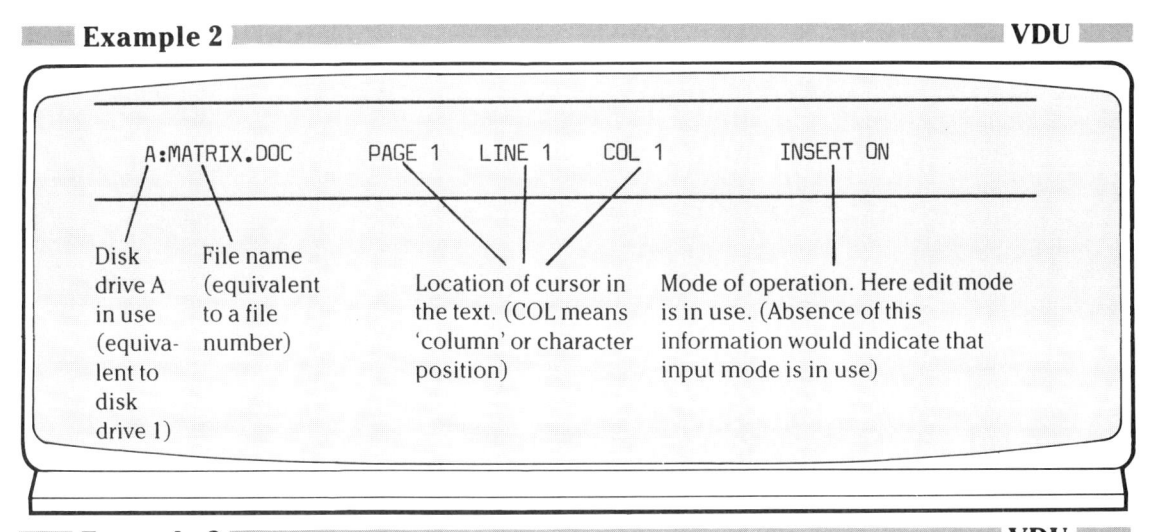

```
            A:MATRIX.DOC    PAGE 1   LINE 1   COL 1        INSERT ON
```

- Disk drive A in use (equivalent to disk drive 1)
- File name (equivalent to a file number)
- Location of cursor in the text. (COL means 'column' or character position)
- Mode of operation. Here edit mode is in use. (Absence of this information would indicate that input mode is in use)

Example 3 — VDU

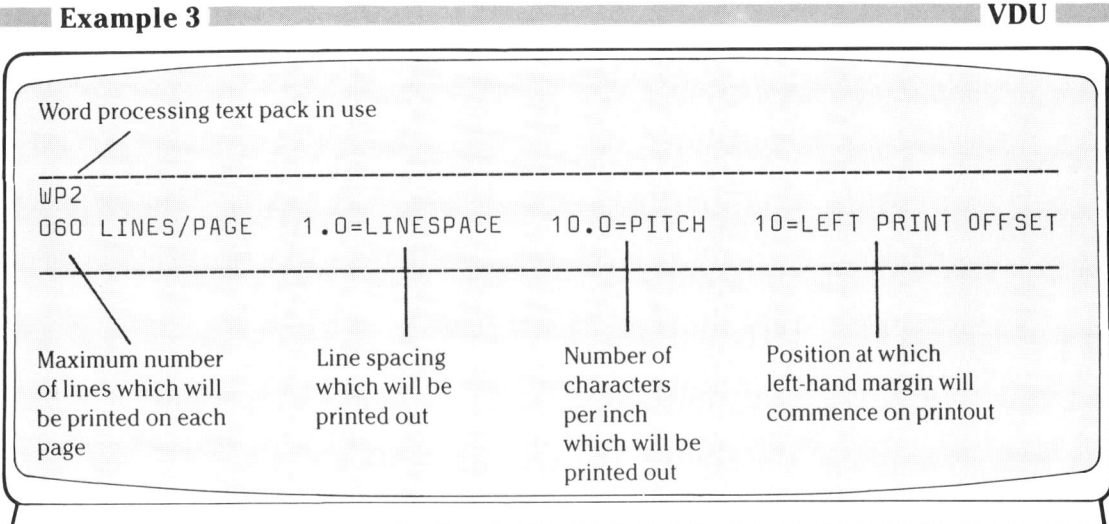

Word processing text pack in use

```
WP2
060 LINES/PAGE    1.0=LINESPACE   10.0=PITCH   10=LEFT PRINT OFFSET
```

- Maximum number of lines which will be printed on each page
- Line spacing which will be printed out
- Number of characters per inch which will be printed out
- Position at which left-hand margin will commence on printout

4.2 Ruler line

This is the second information line to be displayed on the screen, on which margin settings and tab (tabulator) positions are indicated. Again, the style of display will vary from manufacturer to manufacturer. Here are three examples to compare.

Example 1 — VDU

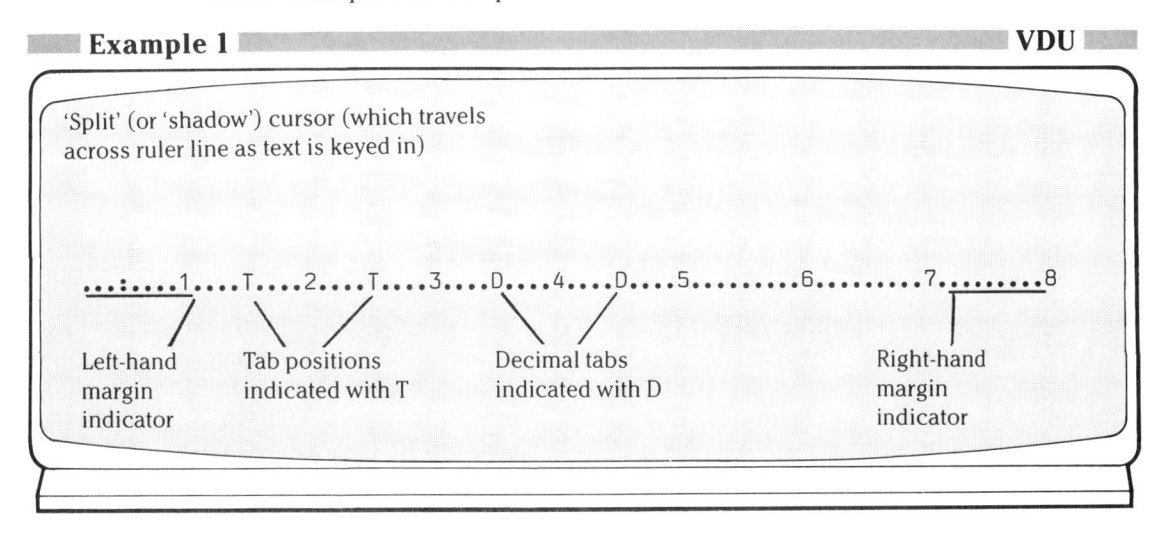

'Split' (or 'shadow') cursor (which travels across ruler line as text is keyed in)

```
....:....1....T....2....T....3....D....4....D....5.........6.........7........8
```

- Left-hand margin indicator
- Tab positions indicated with T
- Decimal tabs indicated with D
- Right-hand margin indicator

Example 2 — VDU

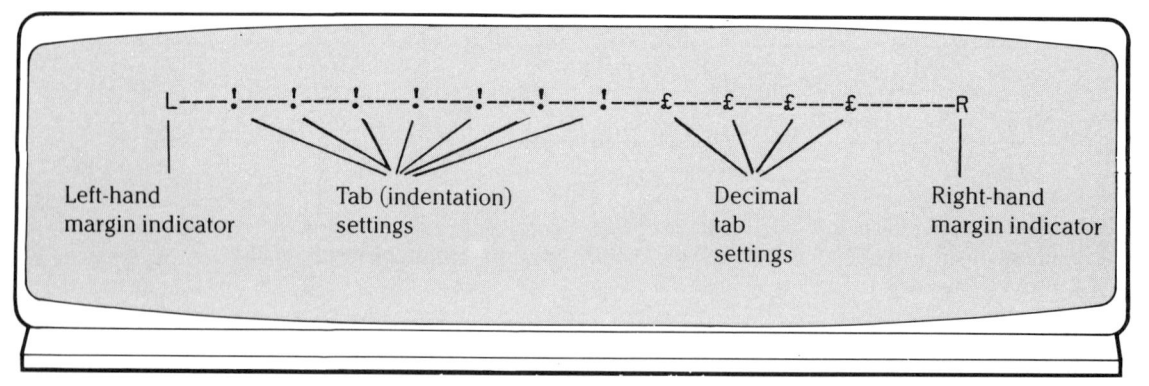

```
L----!----!----!----!----!----!----!----£----£----£----£--------R
```

- Left-hand margin indicator
- Tab (indentation) settings
- Decimal tab settings
- Right-hand margin indicator

Example 3 — VDU

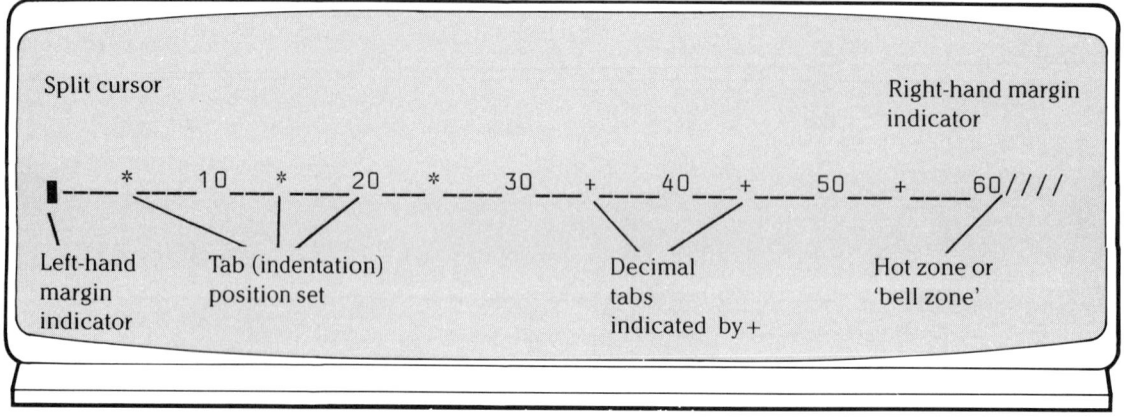

Split cursor

Right-hand margin indicator

```
|----*----10---*----20---*----30---+----40---+----50---+----60////
```

- Left-hand margin indicator
- Tab (indentation) position set
- Decimal tabs indicated by +
- Hot zone or 'bell zone'

In the examples above, tab positions are indicated by exclamation marks, the letter T, and asterisks. Decimal tabs are indicated by pound signs (£), the letter D, and a plus symbol (+). Other manufacturers may use different symbols. Where no tabs are set, the markers are absent. Pre-set (default) settings may be removed easily by the operator, and new instructions can be inserted by giving a simple operating command. Left and right-hand margin settings can be changed easily. The proofreader will need a full understanding of the information displayed on the screen.

For the screenreading exercises in chapter 6 of this book, the following type of status and ruler lines will be used, as in example 2 above.

VDU

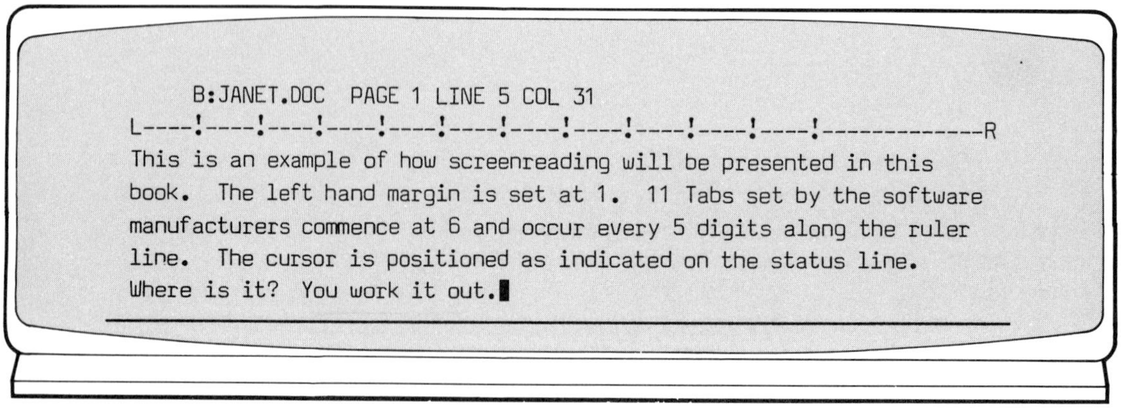

```
     B:JANET.DOC   PAGE 1 LINE 5 COL 31
     L----!----!----!----!----!----!----!----!----!----!----!-------------R
     This is an example of how screenreading will be presented in this
     book.  The left hand margin is set at 1.  11 Tabs set by the software
     manufacturers commence at 6 and occur every 5 digits along the ruler
     line.  The cursor is positioned as indicated on the status line.
     Where is it?  You work it out.█
```

In general, it is important to read through the text carefully when checking it, looking for keyboarding errors and all the points covered in chapter 3. It is good policy to correct mistakes as soon as they are discovered. When dealing with softcopy, attention must be given to the items in this section.

4.3 Control flags and screen symbols

Every system produces symbols on the screen which convey messages to the operator. These symbols may appear in the text, or in a comment line at the side of the screen, or on the ruler or status line, or in a combination of these places. They must be observed as part of screenreading as a whole, and their meaning must be interpreted accurately. Here is a selection of symbols from several systems.

←	Carriage return has been inserted	$\hat{S}$	Word underscore commences/ends
→	Tab has been struck	^O	Space between words has been protected
⇧	Capitals lock is in operation		
⁋	Temporary margin (or coded tab) in use	+b	Bold print instruction commences
		−b	Bold print instruction ends

4.4 Word wraparound

Once the margin settings have been decided (either by the operator, or by using the default), line endings will be taken care of by the machine through its word wraparound facility, without the operator having to use the carriage return key in the middle of a paragraph. Therefore, when screenreading, check that hard carriage return symbols do not appear at line endings, either in the text or in a comment line, where whole paragraphs of text are required. It is especially important to check this when an unjustified (ragged) right-hand margin has been used. In this example, word wraparound has been used.

VDU

```
       A:FACTFILE.DOC  PAGE 1  LINE 5  COL 19
    L----!----!----!----!----!----!----!----!----!----!----!----!------R
    Booting up the system is a technical term which means switching
    on the computer and inserting the system disk.  This term
    originates from the olden-day notion that the day's work could
    not be commenced without first putting on one's boots and
    strapping them up.█
```

Absence of screen symbols shows that correct word wraparound technique was used with this ragged right-hand margin.

In the following example, where word wraparound has not been used, hard carriage return symbols appear in a comment line. This fault could be spotted only on the visual display unit. The symbols will not be printed on the hardcopy.

VDU

```
   A:FACTFILE.DOC  PAGE 1  LINE 5  COL 19
L----!----!----!----!----!----!----!----!----!----!----!------R
Booting up the system is a technical term which means switching    <
on the computer and inserting the system disk.  This term          <
originates from the olden-day notion that the day's work could     <
not be commenced without first putting on one's boots and          <
strapping them up.■
```

Screen symbols indicate that word wraparound was not used because hard carriage returns, inserted by the operator, are recorded by the computer. In this particular example, the screen symbols (or control flags) appear in a comment line

The reason for checking that word wraparound has been used is that, if the draft has to be edited further, paragraphs can be reformed speedily. If a hard carriage return had been inserted, the paragraphs could be reformed only one line at a time, as far as each hard carriage-return. This can be a time-consuming operation.

On most computer systems the hard carriage return screen symbols will be incorporated into the text instead of being in a comment line, and could look like this:

VDU

```
STATUS LINE (displayed in accordance with software program)
RULER LINE (displayed in accordance with software program)

Booting up the system is a technical term which means switching  ←
on the computer and inserting the system disk.  This term        ←
originates from the olden-day notion that the day's work could   ←
not be commenced without first putting on one's boots and        ←
strapping them up.■
```

Carriage return symbols in text

4.5 Hard spaces

When an operator types a space by hitting the space bar on the keyboard, it is referred to as a 'hard space'. Screenreaders should check that every word has a space after it. When a word is punctuated, the reader should check that the space has been placed *after* the punctuation mark. One hard space should be left after commas, semi-colons, colons, and a full-stop when it follows an abbreviation. Two hard spaces should be left after a full-stop when it ends a sentence. Two spaces should be keyed in after an exclamation mark and a question mark when they end a sentence:

I SPACE am SPACE reading SPACE this SPACE example. SPACE SPACE

The reason for inserting hard spaces in the text is to separate words on the softcopy and printout, and to enable speedy text editing operations to be performed whenever the text has to be moved.

Some sophisticated software allows hard spaces to be shown on the VDU by a tiny hidden triangle: ▲ . This makes hard spaces easy to see when a special display light is switched on. As not all software has this facility, the only time some readers will notice the absence of hard spaces is when words are joined together, and when sentences or paragraphs join together after they have been moved.

In the following example, hard spaces were inserted at the end of the paragraphs; if the second paragraph is moved in front of the first one, the display will still be correct.

Correctly displayed copy　　　　　　　　　　　　　　　　　　　　**VDU**

```
STATUS LINE (displayed in accordance with software program)
RULER LINE (displayed in accordance with software program)

Hard carriage returns should not be keyed in at the end of
each horizontal line, in order that word wraparound may
take effect.▲▲ ←
←
The word wraparound feature enables text to be reformed
easily when additions or amendments have been made to it.▲▲←
```

In the following example, hard spaces were not inserted at the end of paragraphs; when the second paragraph was moved up, the two paragraphs joined together.

▬ Incorrectly displayed copy ▬▬▬▬▬▬▬▬▬▬▬▬▬▬▬▬▬▬ VDU ▬

```
STATUS LINE (displayed in accordance with software program)
RULER LINE (displayed in accordance with software program)

The word wraparound feature enables text to be reformed
easily when additions or amendments have been made to it.Hard car←
of each horizontal line in order that word wraparound may
take effect.←
←
```

Hard spaces were not inserted, so there were none to move with the paragraph and the two items have joined together

Screenreaders must check that when new small paragraphs have been formed from one large one, the hard spaces have been left with the last word keyed in, and its punctuation mark.

In the following example, originally all one paragraph, the two hard spaces appear at the beginning of the second paragraph instead of remaining at the end of the first.

▬ Incorrectly displayed copy ▬▬▬▬▬▬▬▬▬▬▬▬▬▬▬▬▬▬ VDU ▬

```
STATUS LINE (displayed in accordance with software program)
RULER LINE (displayed in accordance with software program)

Separate paragraphs may be created by inserting two hard
carriage returns after a full-stop, at edit mode. ←
←
▲▲The hard spaces are then moved along by the computer, to
the beginning of the next paragraph, so to maintain a block
paragraph they will have to be removed by the operator.▲▲←
←
```

Hard spaces still remain, and need to be removed to form a block paragraph

4.6 Soft spaces

These are additional spaces which are inserted by the computer. When a justified right margin is being used, check that the spaces created by the computer do not leave ridiculously large gaps in the text. If such gaps have been automatically created by the insertion of soft spaces, it may be better to alter the layout to a ragged right-hand margin where all the soft spaces will appear at the end of each line, instead of between the words. Small soft space areas are acceptable.

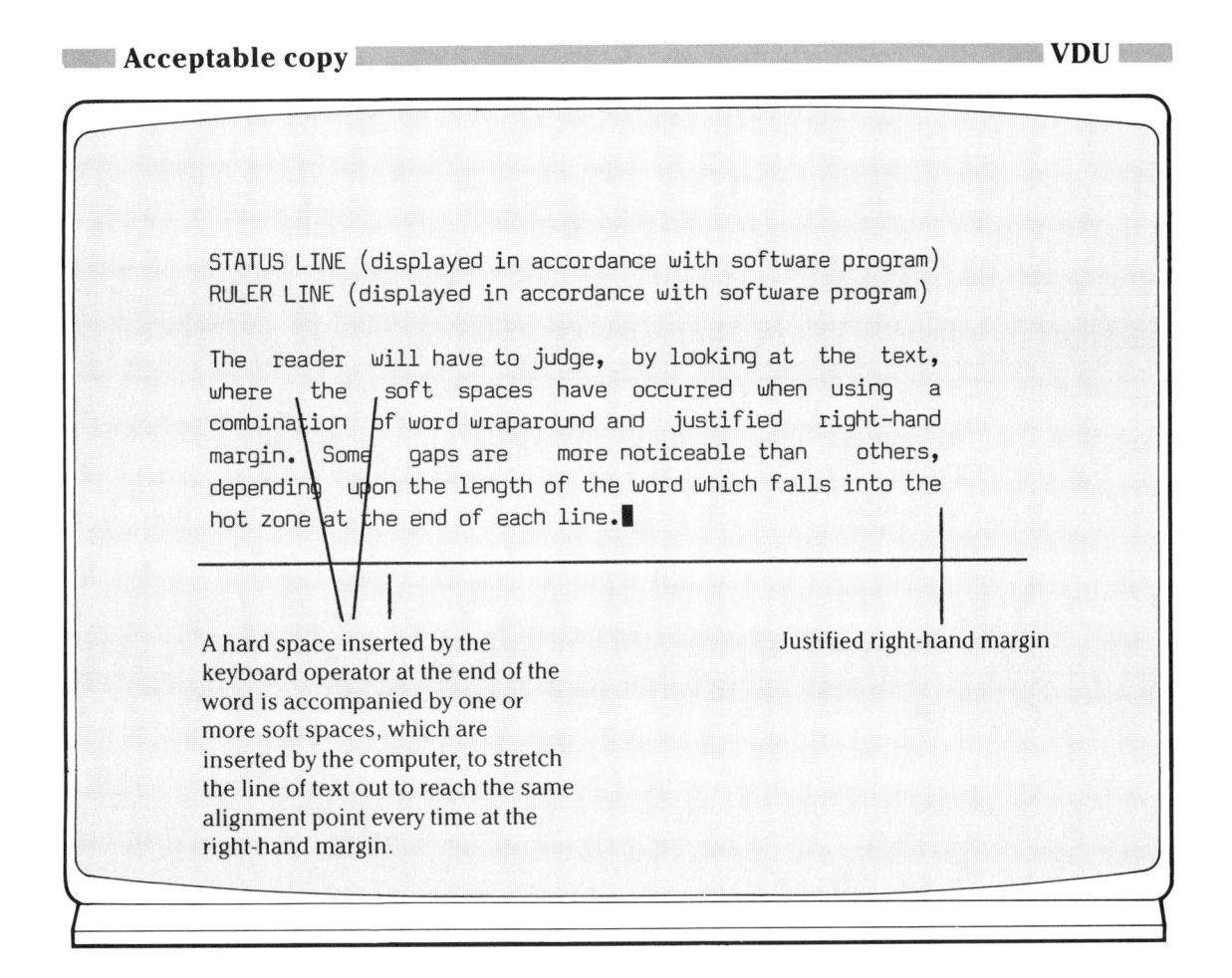

Acceptable copy **VDU**

```
STATUS LINE (displayed in accordance with software program)
RULER LINE (displayed in accordance with software program)

The   reader   will have to judge,   by looking at   the   text,
where   the    soft   spaces   have   occurred   when using   a
combination  of word wraparound and   justified   right-hand
margin.  Some   gaps are    more noticeable than    others,
depending  upon the length of the word which falls into the
hot zone at the end of each line.
```

A hard space inserted by the keyboard operator at the end of the word is accompanied by one or more soft spaces, which are inserted by the computer, to stretch the line of text out to reach the same alignment point every time at the right-hand margin.

Justified right-hand margin

4.7 Protected spaces

Some groups of words should not be divided so that they appear on two lines: the date, people's names, place names, sums of money. Ellipsis dots (. . .) should not be separated from the word to which they belong. Check on the screen that the appropriate command has been inserted which will keep those words together.

Soft spaces inserted by computer

```
STATUS LINE (displayed in accordance with software program)
RULER LINE (displayed in accordance with software program)

At   the   Annual   General   Meeting   of   Waltech   Co   on
30°November°1985, the Chairman, Mr  William  Taylor, said: ←
←
"The  minimum investment is £500 with fees of 5%  now and  a
further 1% later.   There may be   currency   hedging,  but
even°.°.°. if there is not, with a capital growth objective,
the initial yield will be negligible." ←
←
```

Date and ellipsis have protected spaces between the words to keep the word string together.

Justified right-hand margin

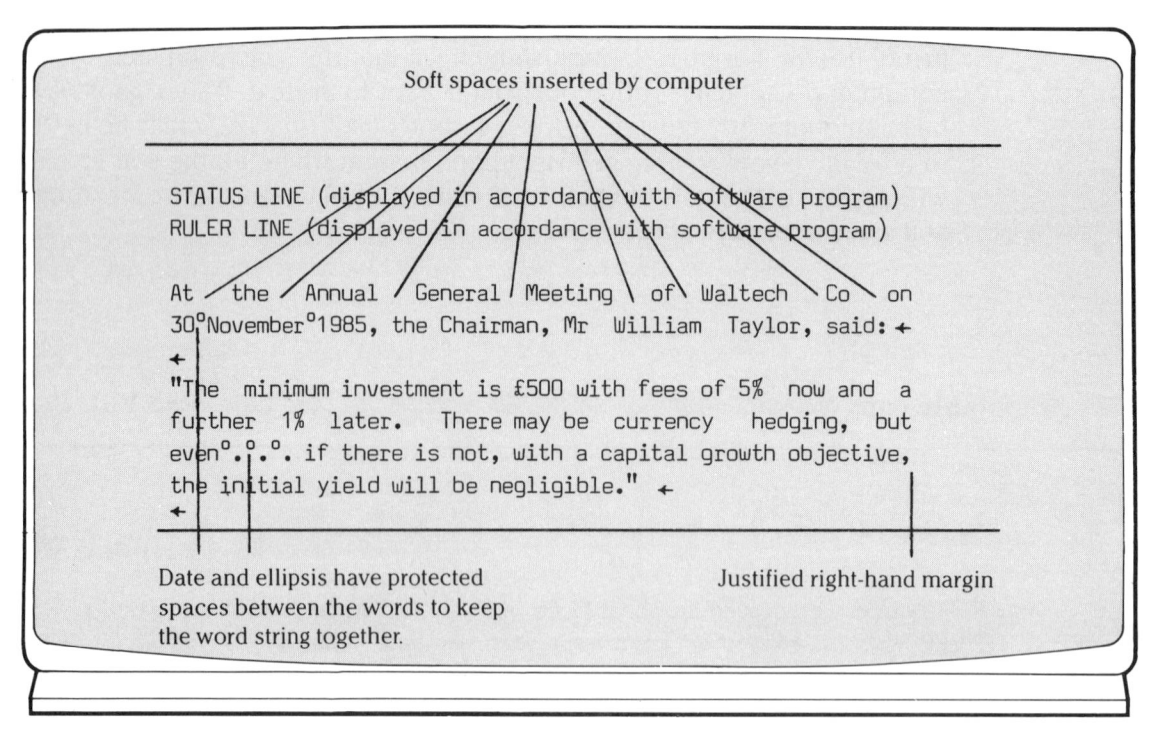

If large soft-space areas occur on the line above (because right-hand justification is being used), it may be better to change to a ragged right-hand margin and reform all existing paragraphs so that soft spaces appear at the end of lines, rather than in the middle.

Soft spaces at end of lines of text

```
STATUS LINE (displayed in accordance with software program)
RULER LINE (displayed in accordance with software program)

At the Annual General Meeting of Waltech Co on
30°November°1985, the Chairman, Mr William Taylor, said: ←
←
"The minimum investment is £500 with fees of 5% now and a
further 1% later.  There may be currency hedging, but
even°.°.°. if there is not, with a capital growth objective,
the initial yield will be negligible." ←
←
```

Groups of words with protected spaces still remain together on one line

Ragged right-hand margin

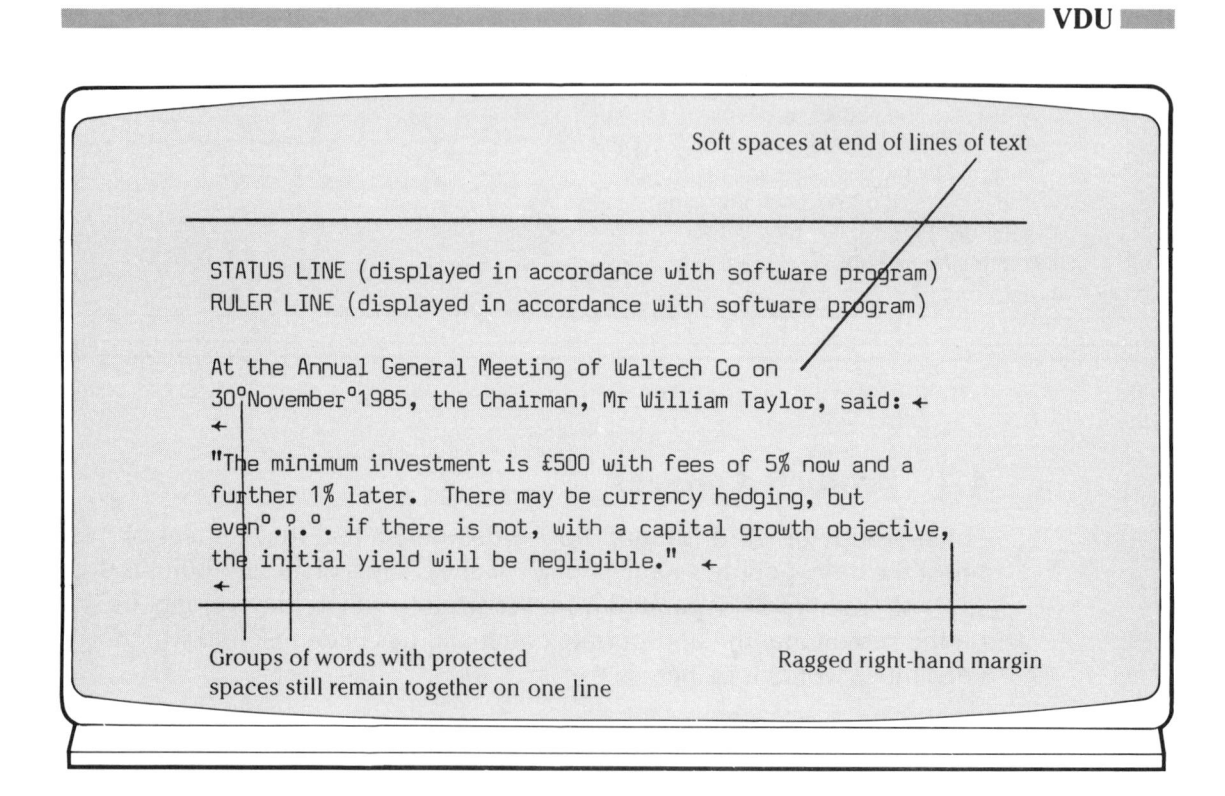

4.8 Reformed text

Check that edited text has been reformed to fit into the margins set.

Insertions   When additional words have been keyed in to the text at edit mode, some word processors may have created space in the text to make room for them:

Original   VDU

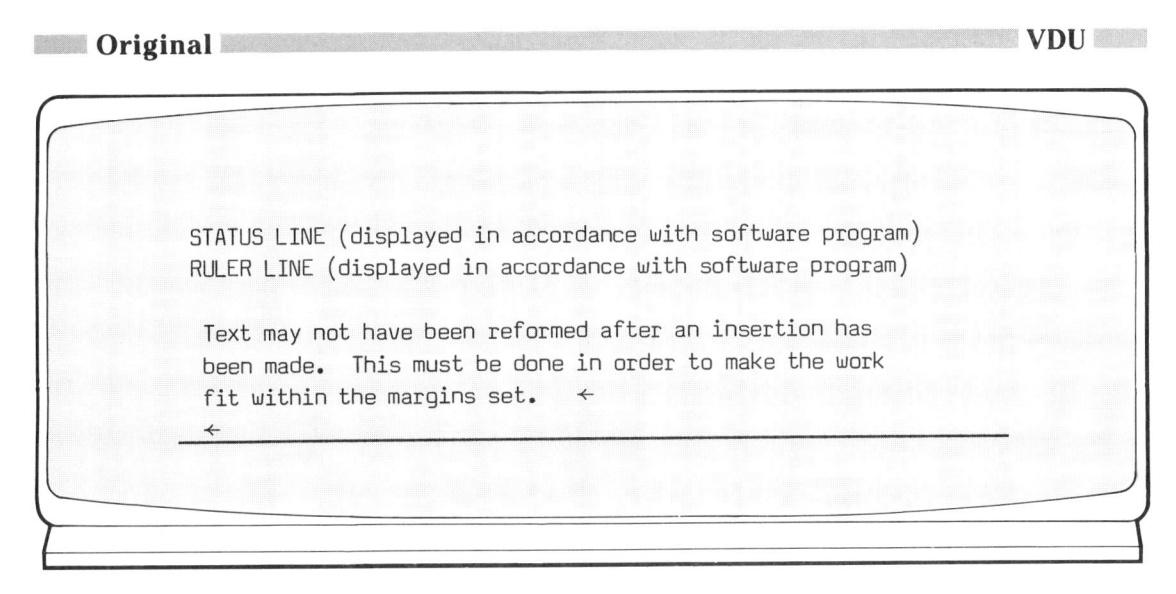

```
STATUS LINE (displayed in accordance with software program)
RULER LINE (displayed in accordance with software program)

Text may not have been reformed after an insertion has
been made.  This must be done in order to make the work
fit within the margins set.   ←
←
```

However, when the words 'or deletion' are added to this paragraph, the screen image could look like this:

Amended version   VDU

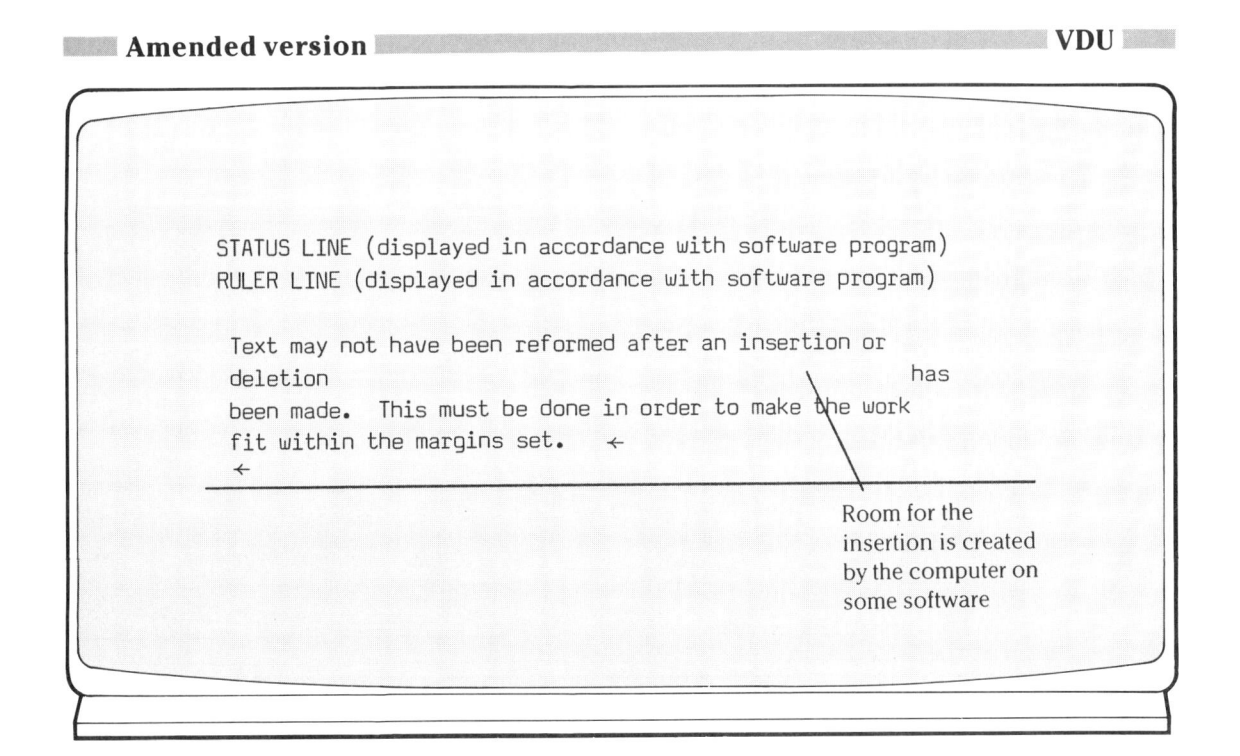

```
STATUS LINE (displayed in accordance with software program)
RULER LINE (displayed in accordance with software program)

Text may not have been reformed after an insertion or
deletion                                           has
been made.  This must be done in order to make the work
fit within the margins set.   ←
←
```

Room for the insertion is created by the computer on some software

An alternative style may look like this:

VDU

```
STATUS LINE (displayed in accordance with software program)
RULER LINE (displayed in accordance with software program)

Text may not have been reformed after an insertion or deletion h+
been made.  This must be done in order to make the work
fit within the margins set.   ←
 ←
```

When the words 'or deletion' were added to the original sentence, in this example the text moved over through the right-hand margin. The screen symbol + indicated that there was more text on the line, which could not be seen on the screen without scrolling. The appropriate command must be given to reform the paragraph before the hardcopy is printed out.

Deletions When deletions have been made, whether a character, a word, or a number of words, the text will disappear. Depending upon the software program, either a space will occur where the text has been, or the right margin will appear to be indented by the number of characters removed from each line.

The following is an example of original text keyed in with a justified right-hand margin.

Original   VDU

```
STATUS LINE (displayed in accordance with software program)
RULER LINE (displayed in accordance with software program)

One method of  removing keyboarded  errors  is  to use the
character delete key.  This key removes text digit by digit
one place to the left of the cursor position.  However, the
use of this key for removing large amounts of text is to be
avoided, as quicker alternatives for deleting are provided.   ←
 ←
```

If the word 'character' is omitted from the second line down, the screen could look like this:

VDU

```
STATUS LINE (displayed in accordance with software program)
RULER LINE (displayed in accordance with software program)

One method of removing keyboarded errors is to use the
          delete key.  This key removes text digit by digit
one place to the left of the cursor position.  However, the
use of this key for removing large amounts of text is to be
avoided, as quicker alternatives for deleting are provided.   ←
←
```

Gap has been created by deleting the word 'character'. The paragraph must be reformed with the appropriate command before a hard copy is printed out

An alternative system may display the deletion as follows:

VDU

```
STATUS LINE (displayed in accordance with software program)
RULER LINE (displayed in accordance with software program)

One method of removing keyboarded errors is to use the
delete key.  This key removes text digit by digit
one place to the left of the cursor position.  However, the
use of this key for removing large amounts of text is to be
avoided, as quicker alternatives for deleting are provided.   ←
←
```

Text has been drawn along to the left margin by the computer, thus leaving a gap at the *right-hand side*

The reader must ensure that the paragraph is reformed before a hard copy is printed out.

4.9 Toggle action commands

It is necessary to check thoroughly that all commands to start a function are cleared when it is no longer required. It is difficult to detect the symbols on the screen when the feature itself does not appear on-screen, but only on the printout. In the following example, the word 'beginning' should be underlined.

VDU

```
STATUS LINE (displayed in accordance with software program)
RULER LINE (displayed in accordance with software program)

An operator who keyed in a specific command at the +Ubeginning
of an instruction may have forgotten to cancel it at the end
and, as in this example, all the words may be underlined in
the printout because the command was not cleared to stop
the underlining feature when it was no longer required after
the word "beginning" on the top line.  ←
 ←
```

Command not cleared at the end of the word 'beginning'

When a toggle command is not switched off, the feature continues to operate. The printout therefore will look like this:

Printout

An operator who keyed in a specific command at the <u>beginning</u> <u>of</u> <u>an</u> <u>instruction</u> <u>may</u> <u>have</u> <u>forgotten</u> <u>to</u> <u>cancel</u> <u>it</u> <u>at</u> <u>the</u> <u>end</u> <u>and,</u> <u>as</u> <u>in</u> <u>this</u> <u>example,</u> <u>all</u> <u>the</u> <u>words</u> <u>may</u> <u>be</u> <u>underlined</u> <u>in</u> <u>the</u> <u>printout</u> <u>because</u> <u>the</u> <u>command</u> <u>was</u> <u>not</u> <u>cleared</u> <u>to</u> <u>stop</u> <u>the</u> <u>underlining</u> <u>feature</u> <u>when</u> <u>it</u> <u>was</u> <u>no</u> <u>longer</u> <u>required</u> <u>after</u> <u>the</u> <u>word</u> <u>"beginning"</u> <u>on</u> <u>the</u> <u>top</u> <u>line.</u>

On some systems, unless both toggles are complete the feature will be ignored entirely.

Other toggle action commands could affect such things as setting and clearing bold print, double-strike, printing out in red, and providing a subscript or superscript.

4.10 Forgotten commands

Some software programs make use of a number of 'defaults'. If the operator forgets to remove or change the 'default', it will not always be spotted on the screen. If, in the following example, the operator was instructed to remove the default which automatically numbers pages, and to use a ragged right margin, then the specific commands should be apparent on the screen. If they have been forgotten, they will be absent from the screen.

Inaccurate screen display   **VDU**

```
STATUS LINE (displayed in accordance with software program)
RULER LINE (displayed in accordance with software program)

Your Ref BB/CD ←
Our Ref  VW/XY ←
←
Date as postmark ←
←
Miss J Taylor ←
134B Westgate Avenue ←
Acomb ←
YORK▲▲▲▲YO2 4LX ←
←
Dear Madam ←
←
PERSONAL SECRETARY ←
←
With reference to your application for the above position,
I should be glad if you would attend for interview on
Thursday, 21 June, at 1400 hrs. Please bring your original
qualifications with you. ←
←
```

Absence of operator's commands indicate that specific instructions have been forgotten

Irregular margin not functioning

Printout on next page.

Therefore the printout will look like this:

Printout

```
                    LETTERHEAD PAPER


Your Ref  BB/CD
Our Ref   VW/XY

Date as postmark

Miss J Taylor
134B Westgate Avenue
Acomb
YORK      YO2 4LX

Dear Madam

PERSONAL SECRETARY

With  reference to your application for the above position,
I should be glad  if  you  would  attend  for  interview on
Thursday, 21 June, at 1400 hrs.  Please bring your original
qualifications with you.

Yours faithfully



Personnel Officer




                              1
```

Letter is given a page number — Justified right-hand margin

Forgotten commands may include such items as

- Forgetting to remove default (or previous) tab stops before setting new ones:

Example 1 Inaccurate screen display

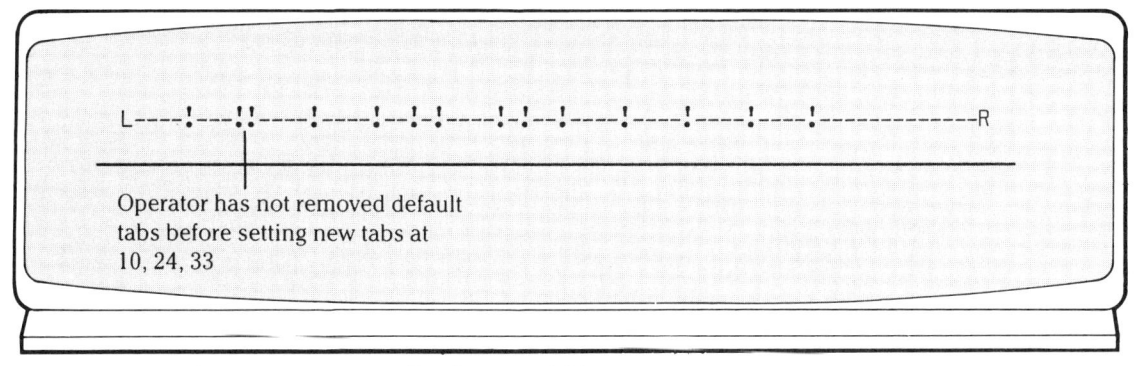

```
L----!---!!----!---!-!-!----!-!--!----!----!----!-----------R
```

Operator has not removed default tabs before setting new tabs at 10, 24, 33

Accurate screen display would be:

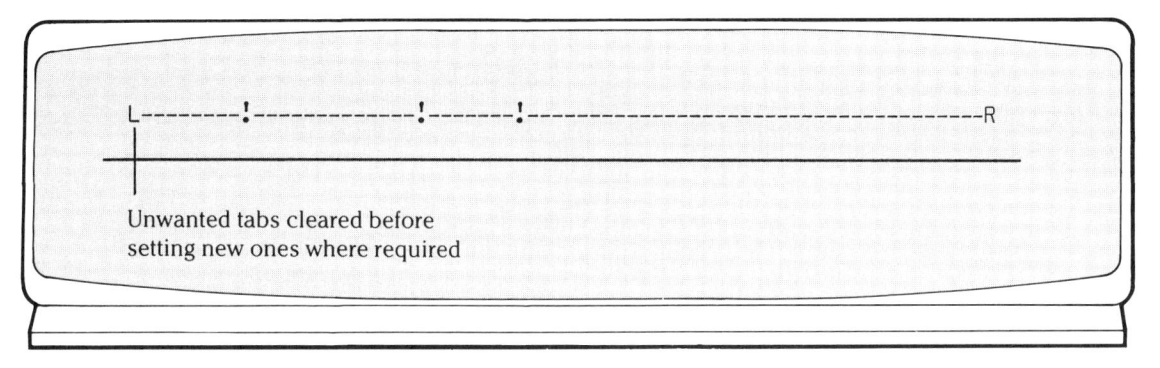

```
L--------!-------------!-------!-------------------------------R
```

Unwanted tabs cleared before setting new ones where required

- Forgetting to use a temporary (or coded) margin:

Example 2 Inaccurate screen display

```
L----------------------!---------------------------R
CAPITAL LOCK KEY      Is a key on the keyboard which puts     <
                      all the letters typed into upper        <
                      case, but has no effect on numbers      <
                      or symbols.█
```

Screen symbols on the right indicate that word wraparound was not used. Therefore the operator must have used the tabulator key on each occasion to reach the temporary margin. Text will be difficult to reform at a later date.

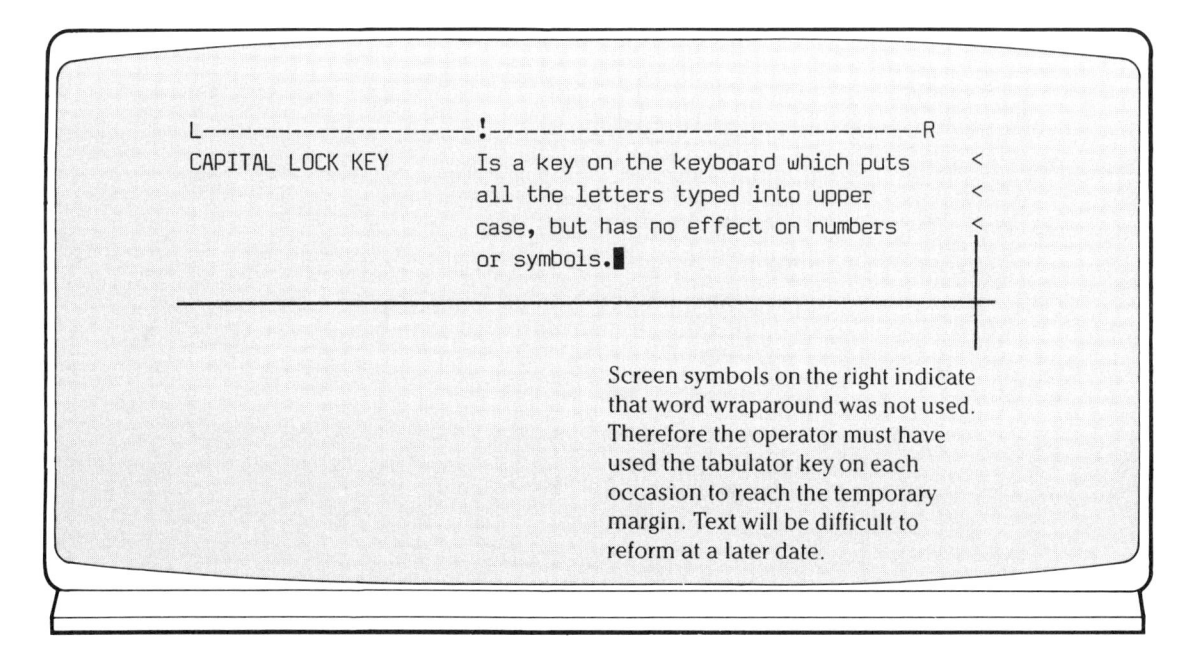

Accurate screen display would be:

```
L▓▓▓▓▓▓▓▓▓▓▓▓▓!--------------------------------R
CAPITAL LOCK KEY      Is a key on the keyboard which puts
                      all the letters typed into upper
                      case, but has no effect on numbers
                      or symbols.■
```

Reverse tone indicates that temporary margin is being used on a tab position

Absence of carriage return symbols in body indicates word wraparound is in use

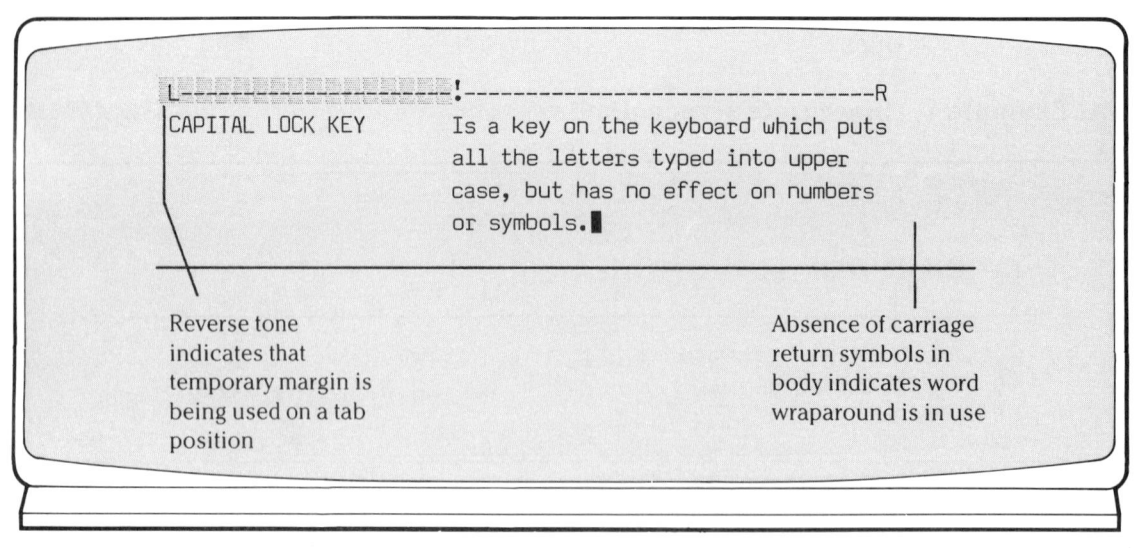

An alternative system may look like this:

Example 3 Inaccurate screen display

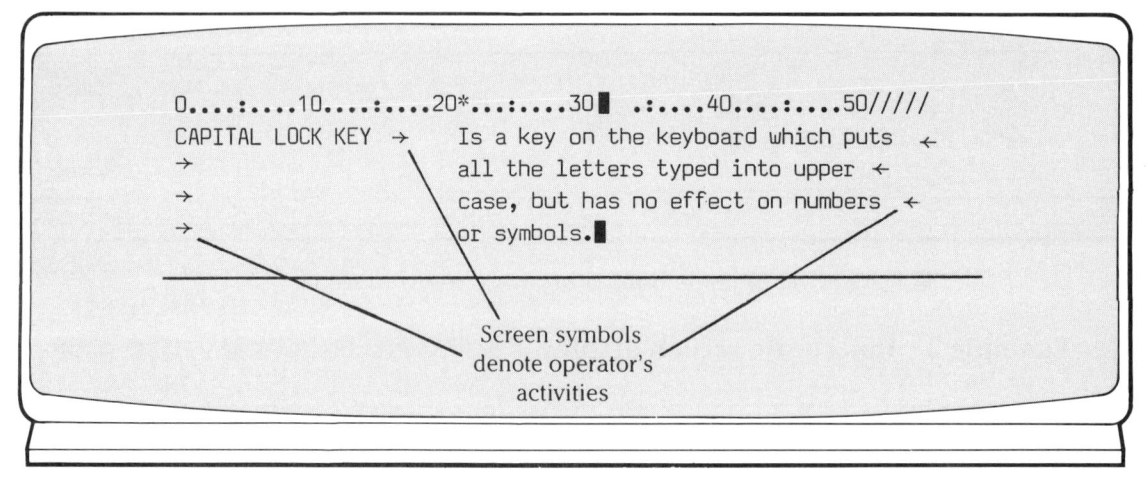

```
0....:....10....:....20*...:....30■ .:....40....:....50/////
CAPITAL LOCK KEY  →   Is a key on the keyboard which puts  ←
→                     all the letters typed into upper     ←
→                     case, but has no effect on numbers   ←
→                     or symbols.■
```

Screen symbols denote operator's activities

Accurate screen display would be:

```
0....:....10....:....20*...:....30■ .:....40....:....50/////
CAPITAL LOCK KEY  →   ■Is a key on the keyboard which puts
                      all the letters typed into upper
                      case, but has no effect on numbers
                      or symbols.■
```

Screen symbol indicates that the appropriate command was used

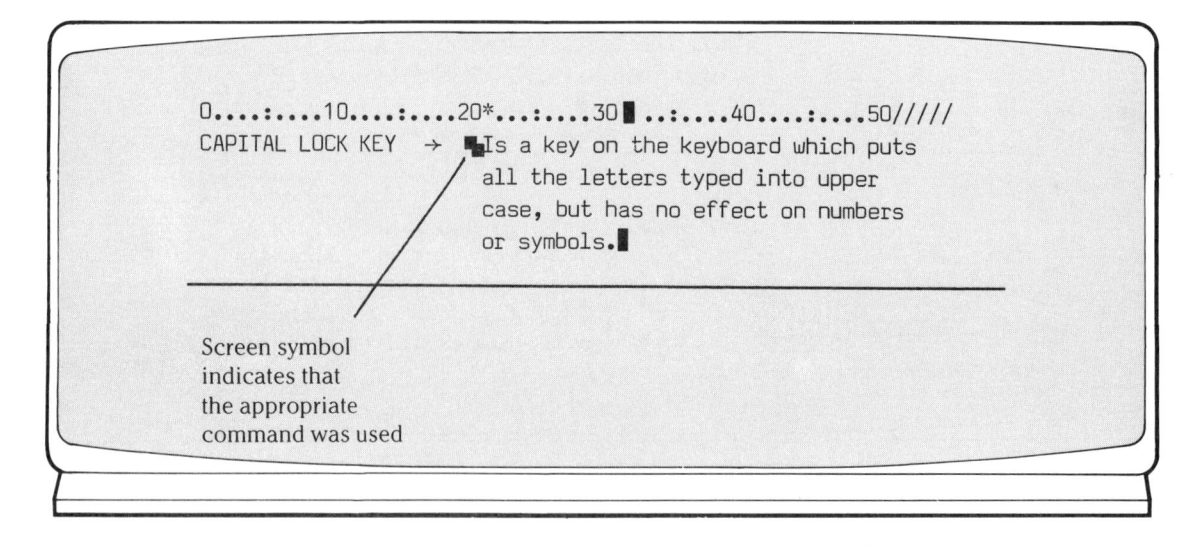

4.11 Misinterpretation errors

There are several other factors to take into consideration when checking for errors on the screen, when the original must always be referred to. Such factors could be *text movement errors*, where information has been moved to another position by the author after the draft has been prepared. In the following example, which looks correct when read in isolation, it will be found that it is incorrect when checked against the original.

VDU

Draft

```
STATUS LINE (displayed in accordance with software program)
RULER LINE (displayed in accordance with software program)

Once a piece of text has been keyed in, the operator may mark
the beginning and end of any amount of it in order to: move
the marked portion, delete it, copy it, write it to disk, etc.▮
```

When the hardcopy had been produced, the originator had asked for the following editing feature to be incorporated.

Printout

Amended draft

```
                Once a piece of text has been keyed in, the operator may mark
                the beginning and end of any amount of it in order to: move
    ⌐⌐          the marked portion,│delete it,│copy it,│write it to disk, etc.
```

Insertion errors occur where new information has been put into the wrong place at edit mode:

Incorrect insertion — VDU

```
STATUS LINE (displayed in accordance with software program)
RULER LINE (displayed in accordance with software program)

Professional proofreaders have their own 'calling terms'
for punctuation and proof correction symbols.  For example,
a full-stop may be referred to as a full-point; a question
mark may be called a query marks or an interrogation mark; a
dash may be referred to as the em-rule (or a 2-em rule) and
an exclamation mark may be referred to as a shriek or a
screamer.
```

When the faircopy was reproduced as a printout, the originator had requested the following amendment:

Amended printout

```
         Professional proofreaders have their own 'calling terms'
marks    for punctuation∧and proof correction symbols.  For example,
         a full-stop may be referred to as a full-point; a question
         mark may be called a query or an interrogation mark; a
         dash may be referred to as the em-rule (or a 2-em rule) and
         an exclamation mark may be referred to as a shriek or a
         screamer.
```

Deletion errors occur where a similar word has been deleted, but from the wrong line or paragraph:

Incorrect deletion — VDU

```
STATUS LINE (displayed in accordance with software program)
RULER LINE (displayed in accordance with software program)

It is negligent for qualified word processing operators to
fail to read through, check and correct their work.  ←
←
Mistakes are often picked up on the hard copy by the
supervisor or a senior member of staff; has to be returned
to the operator, appropriately marked up, and then the text
has to be edited and printed out again.  ←
←
```

The draft was amended to:

Amended printout

It is negligent for qualified word processing operators to
fail to read through, check and correct their work.

Mistakes are often picked up ~~on the hard copy~~ by the
supervisor or a senior member of staff; the hard copy
has to be returned to the operator, appropriately marked
up, and the text has to be edited and printed out again.

Wrong command given to the computer When this happens, a different feature may be carried out; for example, a block of marked text may be copied instead of erased:

VDU

```
STATUS LINE (displayed in accordance with software program)
RULER LINE (displayed in accordance with software program)

UNDERSCORE COMMAND OFFICE PROOFREADING CLEAR UNDERSCORE COMMAND
UNDERSCORE COMMAND OFFICE PROOFREADING CLEAR UNDERSCORE COMMAND

It is the operator's duty to ensure that the work is
accurately checked and corrected BEFORE it is printed out.
```

The command should have been to delete the heading, not to repeat it:

Amended printout

~~OFFICE PROOFREADING~~

It is the operator's duty to ensure that work is
accurately checked and corrected BEFORE it is printed out.

Automatic page breaks not cleared This breaks the text at an inappropriate place, for example after one line of a new paragraph, or when a final line is carried over to a new page:

Incorrect feature — **VDU**

```
STATUS LINE (displayed in accordance with software program)
RULER LINE (displayed in accordance with software program)

operator should therefore refer to the operator's manual for
the particular system being used and to ensure that the
appropriate commands are given for that system.  ←
 ←
Another important feature to observe when checking for errors
---------------------------------------------------------------P
is that widow and orphan lines which have been created by the
computer are rectified by the operator removing the  default.■
```

Page break has isolated one line from the rest of the paragraph to which it belongs. It should be moved up one line so that the whole paragraph is kept together on one page.

4.12 Questions

1. The formatting line at the top of the screen and the ruler line underneath it are i_____ l_____ showing the file name or number, the disk drive in use, and the position of the c_____.

2. Tabulator settings are used for the purpose of i_____ text. They may be indicated by #, T, ★, £ or any other s_____ the software manufacturer has written into the program for this purpose.

3. The carriage return key should not be struck in the course of a p_____ because it cancels out the w_____ w_____ facility, and makes it difficult to r_____ the work when changes have to be made later.

4. One hard space should accompany every word keyed in, except after punctuation marks which end a s_____. When paragraphs have been moved the reader should check that the appropriate spaces have been left with the l_____ word to which they belong.

5. Soft spaces created by the computer may leave large g_____ in the text. Sometimes it is better to remove the right hand j_____ so that all the soft spaces remain at the e_____ of lines.

6   When words are added to an existing paragraph the text already keyed in m_____ o_____ to make room for it. On some systems a gap is created; on others it appears to disappear through the r_____ h_____ m_____.

7   When a toggle-action command has been given, the reader must check that the function has been c_____ when it is no longer required.

4.13 Glossary

comment line A column on some VDUs where screen symbols or control flags appear in a vertical row. This may be called a flag column by some software manufacturers.

control flags (or screen symbols) Markers or symbols < ? F L ↵ which appear on the screen, either in the text or in a comment line, indicating that the operator or the computer has used, or is querying, a function.

cursor A small marker shaped in the form of a rectangle, underline mark, or triangle which indicates the position on the VDU where the next character will be placed in the text at input mode. As information is keyboarded, the cursor moves one character position to the right. At edit mode the cursor indicates the position at which text will be inserted or amended. (*See input mode, edit mode.*)

defaults Preset instructions written into the computer program, such as automatic page numbering, left and right margin settings, tab positions. (Since the machine has to be set to some value, the default value is one which the machine will give in default of any other instructions.)

dedicated word processor A stand-alone computer designed for processing words rather than numbers. It comprises five main parts: a VDU, a keyboard, a central processing unit, a printer and disk drives. Its software has many facilities, a few of which are:

  1 Text may be keyed in, and be temporarily or permanently saved.
  2 Instant corrections can be made to errors.
  3 Deletions, additions and alterations may be made to existing text.
  4 Text may be moved from one place to another.
  5 Documents may be compiled from information already stored.
  6 Specific information (one or more letters or words) may be found, and changed on one occasion only; or automatically changed all the way through the text.

7 Centring is automatic.
8 Line endings may be justified or ragged.
9 Information can be tabulated in columns. There is usually a decimal tab feature where all the characters are automatically positioned around a decimal point as information is keyed in.
10 Information can be merged together from two different memory stores.

edit mode When amendments have to be made to the text, the operator's work becomes editing. Some word processors have a special edit mode program written into the software for this task.

hard carriage return Permanent line-break instruction made by depressing the carriage-return key. This instructs the computer to discontinue the line of text wherever the cursor is situated at the time. (American term: carrier return.)

hard spaces Permanent spaces keyboarded into the text, made by striking the space bar.

hot zone (or bell zone) An area of five or six character spaces immediately preceding the right margin setting. Words keyboarded into the hot zone which are too long to be completed on that line will automatically be carried down to the next line thus enabling word wraparound to take place. (See *word wraparound*.)

incremental printer A printing device which aligns all the spaces evenly between words on the printout.

input mode The state of operation at which text is first keyboarded into the file, page, or document, before editing.

justified right-hand margin Every line of text starts at the same vertical position.

justified right margin Every full line of text ends at the same vertical position.

orphan line The first line of a paragraph which falls by itself at the foot of a page.

protected space A keyed-in space which has been given a specific command to enable a word on either side of it to be kept together on one line.

ragged right An irregular right-hand margin. (The alternative to a justified right-hand margin.)

reformat A computer function which will redesign the original layout once the operator has changed margins, page length etc.

reform A computer function to tidy up, and return to its original style of display, any irregularities in layout which have been created by editing the draft.

reverse tone   On the VDU, the background is normally a darker colour (such as black or dark green) than the images of the characters, which could be white, light green, or orange. With reverse tone, the background becomes the lighter shade and the images are displayed in the darker colour.

ruler line   The information line at the top of the screen on which left and right margin positions, tabulation settings, temporary, decimal, and right-hand tab points and temporary margin stops are indicated.

screenreading   Checking all the information displayed on a visual display unit, including the status and ruler lines, screen symbols, control characters, hard, soft and protected spaces; paragraphs, tabular and document format as well as the accurate keyboarding of the text.

scrolling   A function to move a displayed screenful of text up, down or across.

soft carriage return   The automatic insertion by the computer of a temporary carriage-return command.

softcopy   The information displayed on the VDU.

software   The computer program.

sophisticated software   A powerful computer program which enables a microcomputer to carry out practically all the features of a dedicated word processor.

standalone   A computer which is self-contained. It can be plugged into one electricity supply and is operated by one person at a time. It does not share a central processing unit with any other computer or terminal.

status line   The information line at the top or bottom of the VDU which indicates the disk drive in use, the file name (or number), the line count, column (or cursor) number, page number, and other details.

toggle   An operating command given once to switch a feature on (or off), and repeated to switch the feature off (or on).

visual display unit (VDU)   The television-type screen which contains a cathode ray tube on which information is displayed.

widow line   The last line of a paragraph which falls by itself at the top of a page.

word string   A group of words deliberately kept together.

word wraparound   The automatic feature which enables a keyboard operator to input text continuously without using the carriage return key, so that every line remains inside the area of the margins set. (American term: word wrap.)

5 Proof correction symbols

The British Standard Institution publishes a recommended list of proof correction symbols which are acceptable internationally: British Standard BS 5261: *Part 2 1976 Copy preparation and proof correction*. The list may be bought from BSI or seen at centres such as large libraries and technical colleges in every region. Photocopying is prohibited for copyright reasons, but free use can be made of the details when the standard is being applied, for example in the exercises in this book.

5.1 Proof correction symbols

The following symbols are in general use and should be applied when completing the exercises in the next chapter. Please note that the symbol used in the text is backed up by a mark in the margin.

Instruction	Text symbol	Margin symbol
Insert new matter in the text	∧	New matter followed by ∧
Insert extra matter identified by a letter in a diamond	∧	∧ followed by (for example) Ⓐ◇
Delete	/ through character(s) or ⊢⊣ through word(s)	∂
Delete and close up	⌀ through character ⌸ through word	⌢∂⌣
Do not change	− − − − − − under matter to remain	✓
Transpose characters or words	⊔⊓ around characters or words	⊔⊓

Instruction	Text symbol	Margin symbol
Set or change to capital letters	≡ under character	≡
Set or change to bold type	∿∿∿ under characters	∿
Change capital letters to lower case	Circle characters to be changed	≢
Transpose lines	⌐⌙	⌐⌙
Insert character in superior position	⋋	Y e.g. Ý
Start new paragraph	⌐⌙	⌐⌙
Run on (no new paragraph)	⌒	⌒
Centre	[around matter to centred]	[ ]
Indent	⊐	⊐
Cancel indent	←⊏	⌐

Instruction	Text symbol	Margin symbol
Move matter a specified distance to the right	⌐ around matter to be moved to right ⌐→	⌐⌐
Take over matter to next line, column or page	⌐	⌐
Take back matter to previous line, column or page	⌐	⌐
Close (delete) space between characters or words	linking ⌣ characters	⌣
Raise matter	over matter to be raised / under matter to be raised	⎵
Lower matter	over matter to be lowered / under matter to be lowered	⎴
Correct horizontal alignment	single line above and below	=
Insert space between characters	|	Y
Reduce space between characters	|	↑
Insert space between words	Y	Y

Instruction	Text symbol	Margin symbol
Reduce space between words	⌒	⌒
Make equal space between characters or words	|	Y
Insert space between lines or paragraphs	none	⊃— or —⊂
Reduce space between lines or paragraphs	none	←— or —→
End of correction	none	/

5.2 Questions

What do these symbols mean?

	Margin symbol	Text symbol			Margin symbol	Text symbol
1	✓	- - - - -	6	≡	≡
2	e/	⋌	7	[ ]	[ ]
3	♪	/	8	⊓	⊓
4	♫	⌒ or ⊖	9		⊃— or —⊂
5	≢	○	10	Y	|

6 Practical proofreading exercises

Exercise 1

Correct the draft from the original.

Original

Draft

(a) Thank you for your letter.	Thand you for your litter.
(b) I am coming up to Newcastle in January, and could see you either on the 19th or 20th; please let me know which would suit you.	I am coming up to Newcastle in January, and could see you wither on the 19th or 20th: please let me know which would suit you.

Exercise 2

Correct the draft from the original.

Original

Draft

The company benefited from the 25% reduction on consumable items.	The company benefitted from the 25% reduction on consummable items.

Exercise 3

Without sight of the original, correct the draft.

> Britain has more home computers per head of the population than any other nation. Even though people feel they are missing something if they have no computor knowledge, they believe the machines can be used only by those with a knowledge of mathematics and microelectronics.

Exercise 4

Correct the draft from the original.

Original

Draft

| When Mr Lyle was promoted to work in Timbuctoo, his secretary cried, " I <u>shall never</u> see him again." | When Mr Lyle was to work in Timbuctoo his Secretary cried "I <u>shall</u> see him again." |

Exercise 5

Correct the draft from the original.

Original

Draft

| I believe my friend, Mrs Sheila Einstein, could receive the beige sieve on the eighth of this month. | I beleive my friend, Mrs Shiela Einstien, could recieve the biege seive on the eighth of this month. |

Exercise 6

Correct the draft from the original.

Original

> Home computers cost from around £100, and come with a transformer to plug into the mains. Because it consumes only as much electricity as a 60 watt bulb, it can be plugged into the same adaptor as the cassette player + the TV.

Draft

> Home computers cost from around £100, and come with a transformer to plug into the mains. Because it consumes as much electricity as a 60-watt bulb, it can be plugged in to the same adaptor as the cassette player and the TV.

Exercise 7

Correct the draft from the original.

Original

> Until now, computer manufacturers have pitched their sales campaigns at only part of the market. By appealing to businesses, to men and schoolboys, they have ignored its many uses in the home.

Draft

> Until now, computer manufacturers have pitched their sales campaigns at only part of the market. By appealing to businesses, to men schoolboys, they have ignored its many uses in the home.

Exercise 8

Correct the draft from the original.

Original	Draft
For the purpose of calculating charges for telephone calls between places within the UK and the Isle of Man and within Northern Ireland and the Irish Republic, telephone exchanges are arranged in telephone groups.	For the purpose of calculating charges for telephone calls between places within Northern Ireland and the Irish Republic, telephone exchanges are arranged in telephone groups.

Exercise 9

Correct the draft from the original.

Original	Draft
The basic difference between a home computer and a business computer is that a business computer is designed to handle more information.	The basic difference between a home computer and a business computer is designed to handle more information.

Exercise 10

Without sight of the original, correct the draft.

> Eventually, some files become so packed with
> with papers that they have to be thinned out.
> This is done by taking out the oldest papers
> from the back of the file and transferring
> them to files which are stored out of the cur-
> current filing system; they may still be
> needed for reference, so they should be label-
> clearly, and dated.

Exercise 11

Without sight of the original, correct what you assume to be errors in the draft.

```
1 Jan 1976  — 31 Mar 76
1 Apr  76   — 25 Sep 76
26 Sep 75   — 31 Dec 76
1 Jan  77   — 14 Mar 77
1 Apr  77   — 31 Apr 77
```

Exercise 12

From the accurate total, check the following figures.

```
  2869
  1111
  ————
  9880
```

Exercise 13

Correct the following.

```
The Minster said:
"The text today is taken from One Corinthians
Chapter 13 verse Xlll."
```

Exercise 14

Correct the draft from the original.

Original

Draft

| Our Birmingham branches can be telephoned as follows:

021-455 0002
021-454 6651
021-454 6656
021-454 6671
021-454 6676
021-455 8017 | Our Birmingham branches can be telephoned as follows:

021-455 0002; 021-454 6651;
012-454 6656; 021-454 6771;
021-454 6676; 031-455 8017 |

Exercise 15

Correct the draft from the original.

Original

Draft

| "Looking for errors is fun," said Mary. "I enjoy proof-reading very much and I hope that one day I shall become a Desk Editor in a famous publishing company." | "Looking for errors is fun said Mary. I enjoy proofreading very much and I hope that one day I shall become a Desk Editor in a famous publishing company." |

Exercise 16

Correct the draft from the original.

Original	Draft
(a) The pamphlet is called "Living with Your New Computer", and can be ordered by completing the form below, or by telephone.	The pamphlet is called Living with "Your New Computer", and can be ordered by completing the form, below or by telephone.
(b) She can search through her stock details by manufacturer or by type of garment. The former facility is handy for telling which products sell well, and which don't. Now she can make a switch from one manufacturer to another on the basis of hard data.	She can search through her stock details by manufacturer or by type of garment. The former facility is handy for telling which products sell well and which don't now she can make a switch. From one manufacturer to another on the basis of hard data.

Exercise 17

Correct the draft from the original.

Original	Draft
(a) Other elements — such as silicon — are present in plants, but their presence or availability in the soil is not critical to plant growth.	Other elements - such as silicon are present in plants, but their presence of availability in the soil is not critical to plant growth.

This exercise continues on the next page.

Original	Draft
(b) He has evidence of cardiac abnormality, of peripheral nerve involvement, and of marked cerebellar disturbance.	He has evidence of cardiac abnormality, or peripheral nerve involvement, and of marked cerebellar disturbance.
(c) Jencks, C. et al (1974) Inequality: A Reassessment of the Effect of Family & Schooling in America. London: Allen Lane	Jencks C et al (1974) Inequality: A reassessment of the effect on family and schooling in America London: Allen Lane
(d) The Police made extensive house-to-house enquiries.	The Police made expensive house-to-house enquiries.
(e) One way to determine aim rates is by a comparison with the performance of competent peers or comparisons with a particular pupil's previous levels.	One way to determine aim rates is by a comparison with the performance of competent peers of comparisons with a particular pupil's previous levels.

Exercise 18

Correct the draft from the original.

Original dictation	Draft transcription
The word "matrix" can describe one type of printer in which the letters and numbers are formed by a pattern of dots. An alternative is an "impact printer" where the letters and numbers are printed by some variation on a typewriter mechanism.	The word "matrix" can describe one type of printer in which the letters and numbers are formed by a pattern of dots. An alternative is an "in-packed printer" where the letters and numbers are printed by some variation on a typewriter mechanism.

Exercise 19

Correct the draft from the original.

Original dictation	Draft transcription
The text is first written into the memory of the computer and read on the screen. It can then be refined and corrected; words and paragraphs can be added or deleted or moved around. Substitutions can be made for words or phrases. The text is printed only after editing.	The text is first written into the memory of the computer and red on the screen. It can then be refined and corrected; words and paragraphs can be added or dilated or moved round. Substitutions can be made for words or phrases. The text is printed annually after dating.

Exercise 20

Correct the draft from the original.

Original	Draft
(a) *Possession of a computer would make the study more credible to those whose continuing support is required.*	Possession of a computer would make the study more credible to those who's continuing support is required.
(b) My advice is to find a job in which you can be independent.	My advise is to find a job in which you can be independant.
(c) The Manager, not wishing to lose his game of golf, decided to practise his putting.	The Manager, not wishing to loose his game of golf, decided to practice his putting.

Exercise 21

Correct the draft from the original.

Original	Draft
The Post Office offers a two-tier mailing system.	The post office offers a 2-tier Mailing system.

Exercise 22

Correct these originals.

(a)

The patient's wife says that at times there has been increasing problems with his short-term memory.

(b)

There has already been a great deal of discussion about this project. I and my colleagues are strongly of the opinion that the plan should be put into effect forthwith.

Exercise 23

Correct the draft from the original.

Original	Draft
The telephone number which you require is 01-234 9876.	The telephone number which you require is 01— 234 9876.

Exercise 24

Without sight of the original, correct the draft.

> Our offices are open on weekdays from 9-6; from 9 - 12.00 on Saturdays; and when the sales are on, from 9 to 6 pm each day.

Exercise 25

Correct the draft from the original.

Original	Draft
(a) We are anxious to re-establish the former practice, and shall be glad of your co-operation in publicising it.	We are anxious to reestablish the former practice, and shall be glad of your coopera-tion in publicising it.
(b) Formerly in England the practice of pre-emption was the prerogative of the Sovereign buying household provisions at special prices.	Formerly in England the practice of preemption was the pre-rogative of the sovereign buying household provisions at special rates.

Exercise 26

Correct the draft from the original.

Original	Draft
On Monday, the Physio- therapist was inundated with work referred by Police Constable Paul Fathers.	On Monday, the Physiothe- rapist was inundated with work referred by Po- lice Constable Paul Fat- hers.

Exercise 27

From the three words *argument/augment/agreement*, select the one which best suits the sentence.

[Handwritten: An agreement has been reached between L Saunders and O Cochrane]

Exercise 28

Correct the draft from the original.

Original	Draft transcription
(a) *[Handwritten shorthand]*	Thank you if your letter received. This am we shall be pleased to make an appointment for your ear by next week and suggest Tuesday, 13th, at 10.50 hrs.
(b) *[Handwritten shorthand]*	Thank you for your letter of 7 August. I see you are not about to keep the appointment on the 15th.

Exercise 29

This postcard is to be mailed by the office junior. Before having it retyped correctly, point out the errors. (The junior was asked to write to Mr E Essex, 1 Tenshore Crescent, Louth, Lincs, inviting him to attend for interview on 11th November 1986 at 1315 hours and to mark the communication CONFIDENTIAL.)

```
           OFFICE SUPPLIES LTD        |
           2 HIGH STREET              |
           LOUTH                      |
           LINCS                      |
                                      |
           IO.IO.I986                 |   CONFIDENTIAL
                                      |
Please attend for interveiw on        |
II.II.1986 at I3.I5 hrs.  If          |
this is not conveneint please         |   Mrs E Essex Esq
telephone 0507 I2345 for an           |   IIO Shaw Crescent
an alternative apointment.            |   Louth
                                      |   Lancs
                                      |
                    Manager           |
```

Exercise 30

Indicate the number of obvious mistakes which occur on each line.

1 Thankyou for your telephonemessage.

2 I think that the Agreemint should be singed today.

3 The Minuets will be signed by the Chairmen.

4 These invitations should be printed in our works-
   hops early next week.

5 Voting may be   by a ballet or by proxy.

6 If a convened meeting is postphoned before it is due
   to take place, it is put-off until a later date.

7 A facsimile copy can be taken. On a copying machine.

8 the first Microfilming machine was invented by an
   american bank employee.

9 When ty-ping memos, the top copy is usually typed on
   a printed form called a 'Memorandum.

Exercise 31

Correct these 'originals'.

FOR SALE: FRESHLY CAUGHT CRAB SANDWICHES	NOTICE IN A GREEN-GROCER'S SHOP Due to the drought, leaks are scarce this month.
FOR SALE: QUEEN ANNE STYLE TABLE BY MAN WITH BOW LEGS	The Golconda diamond is 47.29 carrots and has been certified as floorless.
ELECTRIC TYPEWRITER FOR SALE BY WOMAN WITH GOLF-BALL HEAD	These pills are dangerous. Keep them away from children which should be locked in a cupboard.
I bought a fresh salmon for your birthday, but I'm afraid it tasted everything in the fridge.	It is not inadvisable to exceed the stated dosage.

Exercise 32

Find all the mistakes in the following newspaper column.
(Note: Wide spaces are not errors in justified display.)

129 - LOST, FOUND	1 mistake
to the name of Tabby. Reward. Tel 654 3210.	1 mistake
FOUND; Blue bugie. Talks alot. Frequently says "Lets rub his little tum-tum-tum. Box 143.	4 mistakes
GINGER CAR, Captain, lost. Vinder rewarded. Tel 765 4321.	2 mistakes
FOUND: 2 Laddies' necklaces in a presentation bxo. Contact Brown, 234 5678.	2 mistakes
LOST: Mongrel dot named Trudy. Resembles a dash-hound with long legs. Ring: 345 6789.	2 mistakes

127 WANTED	1 mistake
piano. Good condition. Must be in tuna. Offers. Box 147.	2 mistakes
Companionship. Computer manager, 46, separated- tail, rugged-build, seeks to meet lady with varied interests.	3 mistakes

Exercise 33

Rewrite these notices so that they can be read easily.

FIRE NOTICE
Do not destruct the fire doors.

NOTICE
To raise the alarm, break the glass when fire occurs.

SAFETY NOTICE
Keep the gangways clear

STAFF NOTICE
A donkey has been found.
Please contact Office Manager.

WARNING
Please mind your head when leaving your seat.

Holiday Notice
Please notify Personnel Officer of holiday requirements by 2 June.

Exercise 34

Correct the draft from the original.

Original	Draft
At first, the Chairman told shareholders they would receive 50% profit. Later the Chairman told shareholders they would receive only 15% profit.	At first, the Chairman told shareholders they would receive 50% profit. Later the chairman told share-holders they would recieve only 15% proffit.
Professor Cockayne said that Shakespeare's Richard I was well worth seeing at Stratford.	Professor Cockrayne said that Shakespeare's Richard I was well worth seeing at Stafford.
On 31 July the following salary increases will apply: Executives 24% Administrative staff 18% Clerical staff 16% Cleaning staff 5%	On 32 July the following salary increases will apply: Executives 24% Administrative staff 18% Clerical staff 10% Cleaning staff 50%
DIPLOMA FOR TOP EXECUTIVES Applicants must: Hold a degree; or Have passed 2 'A' levels; or Hold HNC or OND in Business Studies; or Be a mature person in need of retraining.	DIPLOMA FOR TOP EXECUTIVES Applicants must: Hold a degree; or Have passed 2 'A' levels; or Hold HNC or OND in Business Studies; or Be a mature person in need of restraining.

Exercise 35

Check the following address, which has been transcribed from an audio machine.

Mr H.A Myatt
18 Glenville Road
SUTTON COLDFIELD
B75 5XW.

Mr H A Wyatt
80 Grenville Row
SUTTAM COALFEEL
B75 58W

Exercise 36

Correct the draft from the original, using the appropriate proof-correction symbols.

Original

WALTEC CO
HOUSERULES FOR TYPEWRITING STANDARDS WITHIN THE COMPANY.

1) Letterhead paper should be used for all out-going letters.
2) Printed memo forms should be used for all internal memoranda.
3) White bond paper should be used for all other work, except carbon copies (use cut bank) and ink duplicated copies (use semi-absorbent paper).
4) Blocked paragraphs should be used throughout.
5) Letters should be fully blocked with open punctuation.
6) Dates should always be in date, month, year order.
7) References should always be Dictator/Typist/file No.
8) Headings should always be in blocked capitals. (No underscore required).
9) Postcodes should comply with Post Office regulations.
10) Attention line must be typed above, the inside address, so that they are correctly displayed when window envelopes are used.
11) Spellings should be checked in a standard English dictionary. Technical words should be checked in an appropriate Technical Dictionary.
12) Words should not be divided at line endings.
13) Typing errors should NEVER be overtyped. Where possible, use the self correcting facility on the equipment available. Otherwise a neatly-painted out error WHICH IS IMPERCEPTIBLE will be accepted.
14) Carbon copies must be corrected properly and corrections made should be as imperceptible as those on the top copy.
15) Catchwords such as Continued... over/ and P/o should not be used.

Draft

```
WALTEC CO

HOUSERULES FOR TYPEWRITING STANDARDS WITHIN THE COMPANY


1    Letterhead paper should be used for all outgoing letters.

2    Printed memo forms should be used for all internal memoranda.

3    White bond paper should be used for all other work, exceot
     carbon copies )use cut bank) and ink duplicated copies (use
     semiabsorbent paper)

4    Letters should be fully blocked with open punctuation.

5    Dates should always be in date, month, year, order.

6    References should always be dictator/typist/file number.

7    Postcodes should comply with Post Office regulations.

8    Attention lines must be typed above the inside address, so
     that they are correctly displayed when window envelopes are
     used.

9    Blocked paragraphs should be used throughout.

10   Headings on letters should always be in blocked capitals.

11   Spellings should be checked in a standard English dictionery.
     Technical words should be ckecked in an appropriate technical
     dictionery.

21   Words should not be divided at line endings.

13   Typing errors should NEVER be overtyped.  Where possible, use
     the selfcorrecting facility on the equipment available.

14   Carbon copies must be corrected properly and corrections made
     should be as imperceptible as those on the top copy.

15   Catchwords such as Continued . . . Over/ and PTO should not
     be used.
```

Exercise 37

Correct the draft from the original.

Original

ENCLOSURE:

ARGUMENTS FOR

1) Nationalisation provides state with an opportunity to control allocation of key resources, e.g. Coal & Steel.

2) Prevents exploitation of consumers.

3) Provides State w. opportunity to control for strategic reasons, operations wh are crucial to national security e.g. power & transport.

ARGUMENTS AGAINST

1) Nationalised industries are insensitive to consumers' needs because of centralised admin.

2) State-run monopoly cd mean th as industry is not subject to market forces, noway consumer needs can be guaged.

3) No profit motivation.

4) An extension of state intervention & public rights infringement.

Draft

Enclosure:

Arguments For

1   Nationalisation provides state with an opportunity to control allocation of key resources, eg coal and steel.

2   Prevents exploitation of consumers.

3   Provides State with opportunity to control for strategic reasons, operations which are crucial to national security, eg power and transport.

Arguments Against

1   Nationalised industrias are insensitive to consumers' needs, because of centralised administration.

2   State-run monopoly could mean that as industry is not subject to market forces, no way consumer ban be guaged.

3   No profit motivation.

4   An extention of state intervention and public rights infringement.

Exercise 38

Correct the draft from the original.

Original

MEMO

To : Mr V McCoy, Personnel Manager
From : Miss Janet Taylor, Production Department
Date : Today's
Heading: Staff Social Club Leisure-hour Competition

I submit the following competition entry:

<u>Aspects of Leadership</u>

Violent acts of picketing,
Brighton bomb – that sort of thing –
Uses leaders of our days
In so many different ways.
Stubbornness will weld ~~but~~ the few;
Dictatorship is nothing new.

Xenophobes, through fear and hate,
Malign, abuse, ~~discriminate~~ intimidate.
Mischievous tongues which whip and snipe
Will label some, like other type
That they have slain, with ~~words~~ and deeds
And turned them into broken reeds.

Proselytisers, in their belief,
Commit their faith, to bring relief.
<u>Their</u> tongues will praise, and raise the will
To do one's best, be better still.
The confidence which <u>they</u> imbue
Brings out the best in others, too.

Leadership, of every kind,
Manipulates the human mind.
The providence of life's rich plan
Affects each type of thinking 'man';
Activists may rule the day,   ACTIVISTS
But surely, <u>God</u> will show the way?

Draft

MEMORANDUM

From   Miss Janet Taylor Production Department *Ref*

To   Mr V Mc Coy Personnel Manager   *Date*

STAFF SOCIAL CLUB LEISURE-HOUR COMPETITION

I submit the following competition entry_

Aspects of Leadership

Violent acts of picketing,
Brighton bomb - that sort of thing -
Uses leaders of our days
In so many different ways.
Stubbornness will weld the few-
Dictatorship is nothing new.

Xenophobes, through fear, and hate,
Malign, abuse, discriminate.
Mischievous tongues which whip and snipe
Will label some, like other type
Tgat they have slain, with plots and deeds,
And turned them into broken reeds.

Proselytisers, in their belief,
Commit their faith, to bring relief.
Their tongues will praise, and raise the will
To do one's best, be better still.
The confidence which *they* imbue
Brings out the best in others, too.

Leadership, of every kind,
Manipulates the human mind.
The providence of life's rich plan
Affects each type of thinking 'man';
Activists may rule the day,
But surely, *God* will show the way?

Exercise 39

Correct the draft from the original.

Original

Mr M Thompson
1123 Exodus Way
Elmfield Estate
NEWCASTLE   NE8 8TQ

Dear Mr Thompson

Mrs Norma Jayne Steel of the Handicapped Work Centre has indicated her desire to join the handicapped persons' 30-week training course being held from 21 September to 6 July.

Before we are able to invoice your Unit with the £10.00 course fee we shall require a signed letter stating that Mrs Steel is in your employ, and that your Unit will pay the fees on your behalf.

We should be grateful if you would forward a letter of authority to us as soon as possible, so that we may offer her a place on the course.

Yours sincerely

Draft

Mr M Thompoon
1123 Exodus Way
Elmfield Estate
NEWCASTLE
NE8 8TQ

Dear Mr Thompoon

Mrs Norma Jayne Steel of the Handicapped Work Centre has indicated her desire to join the handicapped persons 30-week training course being held from 21 September to 6 July.

Before we are able to invoice your Unit with the £1000 course fee, we shall require a singed letter stating that Mrs Steel is in your employ. and that your Unit will pay the fees on her behalf.

We should be grateful if you would forward a letter of authority to us as soon as possible, so that we may offer her a place on the course.

Yours sincerely

Exercise 40

Correct the draft from the original.

Original dictated to audio-typist

"No need to put a reference - I know Thomas very well. However, put today's date in, please.

"The letter is to Thomas Kew Esquire, 22 Stone Road, Leicester, LE3 5JU. Dear Thomas, Thank you for your letter, received this morning. We have now had the outer of kippers despatched to your Agent, as requested. We enclose our invoice. With best wishes, Yours sincerely

Draft

HANTEC KIPPER CO

Soho Road
HULL
HU7 2ET

Tom Askew Esq
20 Twostone Road
LESTER
LE3 SJU

Dear Thomas

Thank you for your letter. Received this morning, we have now had the outer of kippers despatched to your Agent.

As requested, we enclose our invoice with best wishes.

Yours sincerely

Exercise 41

Amend this original and then type the draft.

CAMPING HOLIDAYS IN BRITAIN

WELCOME TO "THE CREAMERY"

Informations and Price

Arriving holiday-makers must stop at office and register. They will be given a numbered plot, and a stickie badge to put on their car.

The office will be open from 9 hrs to 13 hrs for payment of camping fees but reception will be open from 7 hrs to 23 hrs.

TARRIF

Per person (Adult) (each)	£1 per night
Child under 5 years (each)	50p per night
Camping site	50p per night
Tents	£1 per night
Caravans	£2 per night
Autohomes	£1.50 per night
Car	£1 per night
Electricity pluggs	50p per night

Exercise 42

Identify the errors.

```
        A:AUDREY.LET      PAGE 1  LINE 18 COL 54
   L----!----!----!----!----!----!----!----!----!----!-----R
   Date as postmark

   Mr R French
   33 High Street
   NEWCASTLE-ON-TYNE
   NE4 5TH

   Dear Mr French
   I enjoyed meeting you last week, when we had the opportunity to
   discuss your company's proposed plans for a new electronic
   office.

   I confirm that we can supply the MAGICOMPUTER system complete
   with software for word processing, and 5 business packages for
   for wages and salaries; stock control; quality control;
   Magicalc and Magidata at a special discount price of £▮
```

Original

Insert command to prevent letter from having a page number.
Date as postmark.
To: Mr R French, French, Stevens & Co, 33 High St, NEWCASTLE-ON-TYNE NE4 5TH

Dr Mr French

I enjoyed mtg y last wk, when we had the opportunity to discuss your co's proposed plans for a new electronic office.

I confirm th we can supply the MAGICOMPUTER system complete with software for WP, and 5 business packages for wages + salaries; stock control; quality control; Magicalc + Magidata @ a special discount price of £

Exercise 43

This is the revised draft of a speech (below) with its final version (opposite). Check the final version to make sure that all corrections and amendments have been made.

Good afternoon, ladies and gentlemen. I am delighted to be with you all today and feel it is a very great honour to be invited to be your guest speaker on this occasion. When I was invited, by your Chairman, to talk to you about my own personal interpretation of 'The Whitsun Weddings' I felt totally inadequate to even attempt such a task. But, on the other hand, I experienced a great excitement, a joy, that one such as myself had been given the opportunity to express the meaningful impact which 'The Whitsun Weddings' had made upon my reticence. For my inner feelings had been awakened!

My first reactions are that Larkin's work is beautiful. He had a craftsmanlike approach to the portrayal of the English way of life both in this country and in this century. He wrote about England and its people with deep insight, inspiration and genius. Let us take a closer look at what I mean.

In his famous work 'The Whitsun Weddings' larkin himself was travelling on a train from Hull to King's Cross one Saturday at Whitsuntide. When the train pulled out at 1.20 p.m. it was half empty. The windows were down and he sat back in his seat and relaxed. How do we know that he had been rushing? Look at his own words:

["all sense of being in a hurry gone."]

He told how the train ran behind the backs of houses; how the windows reflected the sunlight; how he could smell the fish-dock of Hull and observed the Humber drifting along, and he painted a picture of the horizon, showing where sky and land and water join. All afternoon, through the heat, the train curved southwards, stopping at stations, making the journey tediously slower.

Please retain this thumb space. Also check the spelling of 'all right'. I'm not sure whether it should be 'alright'.

Good afternoon, ladies and gentlemen. I am delighted to be with you all today and feel it is a very great honour to be invited to be your guest speaker on this occasion. When I was invited, by your Chairman, to talk to you about my own personal interpretation of 'The Whitsun Weddings' I felt totally inadequate even to attempt such a task. But, on the other hand, I experienced a great excitement, a joy, that one such as myself had been given the opportunity to express the meaningful impact which 'The Whitsun Weddings' had made upon my reticence. For my inner feelings had been awakened!

My first reactions are that Larkin's work is beautiful. He had a craftsmanlike approach to the portrayal of the English way of life both in this country and in this century. He wrote about England and its people with deep insight, inspiration and genius. Let us take a closer look at what I mean.

In his famous work 'The Whitsun Weddings' Larkin himself was travelling on a train from Hull to King's Cross one Saturday at Whitsuntide. When the train pulled out at 1.20 pm it was half empty. The windows were down and he sat back in his seat and relaxed. How do we know that he had been rushing? Look at his own words:

"all sense of being in a hurry gone."

He told how the train ran behind the backs of houses; how the windows reflected the sunlight; how he could smell the fish-dock of Hull and observed the Humber drifting along, and he painted a picture of the horizon, showing where sky and land and water join. All afternoon, through the heat, the train curved southwards, stopping at stations, making the journey tediously slower.

(over)

Exercise 43 continued

He described how farms went by; how cattle stood in the fields, casting short shadows because of the height of the sun in the sky; how canals could be seen carrying their effluent. A greenhouse reflected the sun's rays in such a way he'd never seen before. The optical illusion of hedges dipping and rising almost made me feel I was a passenger on the same train!

Now and then the smell of grass wafted in through the open windows, temporarily replacing the odour of the worn seats, and then the next town appeared with its scrap yards of discarded vehicles.

In first two verses Larkin set the scene magnificently. He used few words to convey a very large meaning. He gave a lot of information about things by selecting for us the really relevant details. We not only saw the picture as he painted it, but we smelt it, too. And we almost heard the wheels on the lines, and felt the heat of the sunlight. We somehow sensed that it was going to be a long, hot, tedious journey. But, in addition, he was raising our awareness. In some uncanny way he was preparing us for some kind of activity which was occurring. Look at the subtlety of the words:
"At first, I didn't notice what a noise the weddings made".

He almost made us feel unobservant too. If he didn't notice the noise, how could we? He had been so pre-occupied with the landscape and all that was in it, he hadn't realised what was being on on the platform, so he tried to justify his lack of
observation by pointing out that it was not easy to see
what was happening in the shade. He had assumed the
noises were being made by station staff handling the
mail. Now, on that occasion, as the train left
the station, he noticed people remaining on the
platform, grinning, and over-dressed in the

He described how farms went by; how cattle stood in the fields, casting short shadows because of the height of the sun in the sky; how canals could be seen carrying their effluent. A greenhouse reflected the sun's rays in such a way he'd never seen before. The optical illusion of hedges dipping and rising almost made me feel I was a passenger on the same train!

Now and then the smell of grass wafted in through the open windows, temporarily replacing the odour of the worn seats, and then the next town appeared with its scrap yards of discarded vehicles.

In these first two verses Larkin set the scene magnificently. He used few words to convey a very large meaning. He gave a lot of information about things by selecting for us the really relevant details. We not only saw the picture as he painted it, but we smelt it, too. And we almost heard the wheels on the lines, and felt the heat of the sunlight. Somehow we sensed that it was going to be a long, hot, tedious journey. But, in addition, he was raising our awareness. In some uncanny way he was preparing us for some kind of activity which was occurring. Look at the subtlety of the words:

"At first, I didn't notice what a noise the weddings made".

He almost made us feel unobservant too. If he didn't notice the noise, how could we? He had been so pre-occupied with the landscape and all that was in it, he hadn't realised what was going on on the platform, so he tried to justify his lack of
    observation by pointing out that it was not easy to see
        what was happening in the shade. He had assumed the
            noises were being made by station staff handling the
                mail. Now, on that occasion, as the train left
                    the station, he noticed people remaining on the
                        platform, grinning, and over-dressed in the

(over)

Exercise 43 continued

fashions of the day, especially the girls in high-heeled shoes and veiled hats, and they appeared to be waving goodbye. His curiosity aroused, he became interested so at the next station he stuck his head out of the window - and saw exactly the same type of thing happening again. This time he digested the situation! He realised that these people who remained were the guests of wedding parties who had come to the station to wave off the newly married couple. Oh, how his eyes observed the people! Notice how he was particularly drawn to the fathers. He noticed the mothers, too. Isn't it amazing, even in those days, that mothers tended to be fat? We think of obesity as one of today's ailments but Larkin showed that it has been there for decades. He noticed the Uncles telling smutty stories. Then the attention went to the women's permed hair. Suddenly the narration of an everyday scene became deeply meaningful. The women did not wear green, purple or yellow dresses. No. The subtleties were expanded to "lemons, mauves and olive ochres" and even the pieces of jewellery they wore were noted to be cheap substitutes. He sorted out, too, the age groups in the parties and noticed that not everyone had arrived at the station. From his vantage point in the train he could see wedding parties leaving street cafés; banquetting halls up yards; and public houses which had bunting in the coach parks. Certainly I could imagine that I could see it too! It was like being on the train myself.

Then his mood changed to a nostalgic one. All down the route fresh couples climbed aboard, leaving their guests on the platform until the last couple had taken their place on the train. When he realised that the last of the confetti, and advice, had been thrown the couple's way, he looked at the faces of the people he could see and tried to read their minds.
He sat back in his seat and reflected on all which he had seen. He wondered why some of the children were frowning. He compared the faces of the fathers (showing that everything had gone off all right)

3

fashions of the day, especially the girls in high-heeled shoes and veiled hats, and they appeared to be waving goodbye. His curiosity aroused, he became interested so at the next station he stuck his head out of the window - and saw exactly the same type of thing happening again. This time he digested the situation! He realised that these people who remained were the guests of wedding parties who had come to the station to wave off the newly married couple. Oh, how his eyes observed the people! Notice how he was particularly drawn to the fathers. He noticed the mothers, too. Isn't it amazing, even in those days, that mothers tended to be fat? We think of obesity as one of today's ailments but Larkin showed that it has been there for decades. He noticed the Uncles telling smutty stories. Then the attention went to the women's permed hair. Suddenly the narration of an everyday scene became deeply meaningful. The women did not wear green, purple or yellow dresses. No. The subtleties were expanded to "lemons, mauves and olive ochres" and even the pieces of jewellery they wore were noted to be cheap substitutes. He sorted out, too, the age groups in the parties and noticed that not everyone had arrived at the station. From his vantage point in the train he could see wedding parties leaving street cafés; banqueting halls up yards; and public houses which had bunting in the coach parks. Certainly I could imagine that I could see it too! It was like being on the train myself.

Then his mood changed to a nostalgic one. All down the route fresh couples climbed aboard, leaving their guests on the platform until the last couple had taken their place on the train. When he realised that the last of the confetti, and
    advice, had been thrown the couple's way, he looked at the faces of the people he could see and tried to read their minds.
        He sat back in his seat and reflected on all which he
            had seen. He wondered why some of the children were
                frowning. He compared the faces of the fathers
                    (showing that everything had gone off all right)

(over)

Exercise 43 continued

with the women's faces, streaked with tears. Perhaps they were tears of happiness; perhaps an inward reflection of their own wedding day; perhaps they felt they had just 'lost' a son or a daughter; and this reminded him of a funeral rather than a wedding. He reminisced about how girls held their handbags tightly and stared into space. Perhaps they were thinking of the consummation that night would bring - how tonight it would be all right because now the couple had the Church's blessing to go ahead. Now the act of sex had been sanctified by religious rites and legal ceremony. Was it possible that those girls were jealous? Certainly something showed in their faces!

Suddenly the narrator felt an involved outsider. He tried to detach himself from the situation by returning to give a further description of the scene. Perhaps he felt embarrassed by his own penetrating thoughts? To avert his involvement, he looked at his watch and realised that in 50 minutes they would reach their destination. As he relaxed his mind wandered back to the situation in which he found himself - and he felt in limbo. He was half watching the scenery - an Odeon cinema, a cooling tower, a cricket match - yet at the same time he was reflecting on life's meaning. Just imagine. On that journey alone, 12 marriages had got under way!

We gained the impression that to a certain extent Larkin was saddened by the fact that none of those people seemed to care for anyone or anything else. They were not bothered about the people they didn't know. But he was sensitive. He saw the reality of life, its purpose and its meaning and he thought about the increase in the population those marriages would bring. He related it to the population of London and the flatness of the people (just as L. S. Lowry's people are shown as flat images with no personalities; no depth of character) and he imagined them set out in a map-like significance, like fields of wheat spread out. Was he,

4

with the women's faces, streaked with tears. Perhaps they were tears of happiness; perhaps an inward reflection of their own wedding day; perhaps they felt they had just 'lost' a son or a daughter; and this reminded him of a funeral rather than a wedding. He reminisced about how girls held their handbags tightly and stared into space. Perhaps they were thinking of the consummation that night would bring - how that night it would be all right because now the couple had the Church's blessing to go ahead. Now the act of sex had been sanctified by religious rites and legal ceremony. Was it possible that those girls were jealous? Certainly something showed in their faces!

Suddenly the narrator felt an involved outsider. He tried to detach himself from the situation by returning to give a further description of the scene. Perhaps he felt embarrassed by his own penetrating thoughts? To avert his involvement, he looked at his watch and realised that in 50 minutes they would reach their destination. As he relaxed his mind wandered back to the situation in which he found himself - and he felt in limbo. He was half watching the scenery - an Odeon cinema, a cooling tower, a cricket match - yet at the same time he was reflecting on life's meaning. Just imagine. On that one journey alone, 12 marriages had got under way!

We gained the impression that to a certain extent Larkin was saddened by the fact that none of those people seemed to care for anyone or anything else. They were not bothered about the people they didn't know. But he was sensitive. He saw the reality of life, its purpose and its meaning and he thought about the
   increase in the population those marriages would bring. He
      related it to the population of London and the flatness of the
         people (just as L S Lowry's people are shown as flat images
           with no personalities; no depth of character) and he
             imagined them set out in a map-like significance,
               like fields of wheat spread out. Was he,

(over)

Exercise 43 continued

Perhaps ~~he was~~ thinking of bread being the staff (stave) of life and people being the staff (personnel) of life?

In the last verse the journey was drawing to an end ~~and~~ Larkin pondered about life-through-to-death. For some reason he thought it too much of a coincidence that they were all travelling together - there must be a reason for it somehow. As the train slowed down, everyone moved into the corridor. Looking at the ages of those present today, I don't suppose there are many of you here who remember the thrusting motion of commuters on steam train journeys during the war years. Trains were so full that the corridors were packed with people and luggage. Soldiers and civilians ~~used to be~~ compressed in the corridors looked like the shaft of an arrow; the head of the arrow being formed by all those people standing in the vestibule of the carriage. ~~There was even one train called the 'Golden Arrow'.~~ As the train ~~braked~~ the people in the corridors surged forwards. When the train lurched towards a standstill, they fell backwards. Sometimes they would sway forwards and backwards several times, depending on the rate of deceleration of the train; then the people in the vestibule would fall over their luggage in a shambles of disarray.

I believe that Larkin was comparing this thrusting motion of a stream of people, with the marital activity which fulfils a promise to God to go forth and bear fruit, and the breaking up of the arrow head like an arrow shower is therefore most significant.

For me, 'The Whitsun Weddings' has brought understanding and enrichment into my life. This perceptive chronicler of our times through his fantastic skill and ability, has certainly aroused my awareness in poetry. I hope his work will enthral you, too, and the children you teach.

(I know the second 'l' is optional, but I think we'll leave it out!)

5

perhaps, thinking of bread being the staff (stave) of life and people being the staff (personnel) of life?

In the last verse the journey was drawing to an end and Larkin pondered about life-through-to-death. For some reason he thought it too much of a coincidence that they were all travelling together - there must be a reason for it somehow. As the train slowed down, everyone moved into the corridor. Looking at the ages of those present today, I don't suppose there are many of you here who remember the thrusting motion of commuters on steam train journeys during the war years. Trains were so full that the corridors were packed with people and luggage. Soldiers and civilians compressed in the corridors looked like the shaft of an arrow; the head of the arrow being formed by all those people standing in the vestibule of the carriage. As the train braked the people in the corridors surged forwards. When the train lurched towards a standstill, they fell backwards. Sometimes they would sway forwards and backwards several times, depending on the rate of deceleration of the train; then the people in the vestibule would fall over their luggage in a shambles of disarray.

I believe that Larkin was comparing this thrusting motion of a stream of people, with the marital activity which fulfils a promise to God to go forth and bear fruit, and the breaking up of the arrow head like an arrow shower is therefore most significant.

> For me, 'The Whitsun Weddings' has brought understanding and enrichment into my life. This perceptive chronicler of our times through his fantastic skill and ability, has certainly aroused my awareness in poetry. I hope his work will enthral you, too, and the children you teach.

(end)

Exercise 44

Identify the errors.

```
     A:DONNA.LET      PAGE 2  LINE 4  COL 2
L----!----!----!----!----!----!----!----!----!----!------R
and   I  am  confident  that  now we shall be able to    convince
you    that  our product  is the finest  in the  land  and  hope
that  you  will take  advantage  of this  very  special offer .
.■                                                              ?
```

and I am confident that now/we shall be able to convince you that our product is the finest in the land and hope that you will take advantage of this very special offer . . .

Exercise 45

Identify the mistakes.

The operator was told to underline and centre the headings.

```
     A:AUDREY.REP      PAGE 1  LINE 3  COL 1
L----!----!----!----!----!----!----!----!----!----!------R
REPORT
■
```

Exercise 46

Identify the error.

```
A:ISOBEL.TLK      PAGE 1  LINE 14  COL 1
L----!----!----!----!----!----!----!----!----!----!----!-----R
   Good afternoon, Ladies and Gentlemen.  Having been asked  to
   look at  the specific aspects of the enigma of the   commercial
   teacher,  my  thoughts immediately turned to an incident which
   happened to me a number of years ago.  Having just put  a  5p
   coin  into a photocopier,  the copy started to protrude in the
   normal  way  and then suddenly,  without warning, the  machine
   revved up at breakneck speed and out shot three yards of paper,
   followed  meekly  by  the final paragraph of the sheet  I  was
   copying, making the photocopy 9 ft 3 in (2.82 metres) long.Now dra+
   howled with laughter . . . and then tried again  and a similar
   incident  occurred,  only  this  time  the  zinc coated  paper
   remained  short of its previous performance - this time it was
   only 6 ft 3 in (1.91 metres) long.                              <
```

Original

Good afternoon, Ladies & Gentlemen. Having been asked to look at the specific aspects of the enigma of the commercial teacher, my thoughts immediately turned to an incident which happened to me a number of years ago. Having just put a 5p coin into a photocopier, the copy started to protrude in the normal way and then suddenly, without warning, the machine revved up at breakneck speed and out shot 3 yards of paper, followed meekly by the final paragraph of the sheet I was copying, making the photocopy 9'3" (2.82m) long. I howled with laughter ... and then tried again & a similar incident occurred, only this time the zinc coated paper remained short of its previous performance - this time it was only 6'3" (1.91m) long.

(Now dramatically reveal the genuine photocopy and allow time for a reaction before proceeding.)

Exercise 47

Identify the errors.

```
        A:AUDREY.CON   PAGE 1  LINE 1  COL 1   INSERT ON  LINE SPACING 2
L----!----!----!----!----!----!----!----!----!----!----!------R
■H I S   C O N V E Y A N C E   is made the * of *

BETWEEN * of * and * of * (hereinafter called "the Vendors

of the one part and * of * (hereinafter called "the

purchaser" of the other part -------------------------------
```

Original

Please use double-line spacing

THIS CONVEYANCE is made the *
day of * BETWEEN * of * and
* of * (hereinafter called "the Vendors"
of the one part). and * of *
(hereinafter called 'the Purchaser")
of the other part --------

Operator

Please put THIS CONVEYANCE in spaced capitals

Exercise 48

Check the screen image with the manuscript supplied.

```
A:AUDREY.MEM         PAGE 1  LINE 9  COL 1
L----!----!----!----!----!----!----!----!----!----!----!------R
To all Word Processing Operators                             <
From Word Processing Supervisor                              <
                                                             <
I am concerned about the cconomy of stationary and I
particularly ask your cooperation with regard to the saving of
listing paper.It seems that there is an excessive wate and I
would like you to conserve stocks whereever possible.        <
                                                             <
```

Original

Remove automatic page numbering.
Date the memo tomorrow, please.

To all WP Operators
From WP Supervisor

I am concerned about the economy of stationery and I particularly ask yr co-operation w regard to the saving of listing paper. It seems th. there is an excessive waste and I should like you to conserve stocks wherever possible.

Exercise 49

Identify the mistakes.

```
   B:DAVID.CIR       PAGE 1  LINE 13  COL 63
!-------------------------------!------------------------R
I shall be glad if you will let me have your holiday
arrangements for the current year.  Please return the bottom
portion of this letter +USas soon as possible. ←
→
---------------------------------------------------------- ←

I expect to be on holiday from →  ........................... ←

I expect to return to work on →  ........................... ←

Signed ......................▲▲▲▲▲Date ..................... ←

department →                     ..........................
```

Original

> I shall be glad if y wl let me have your holiday arrangements for the current year. Please return the bottom portion of this letter <u>a.s.a.p.</u>
>
> ------------------------------
>
> I expect to be on holiday from ....
> I expect to return to work on ....
> Signed .... Date ....
> Department ....

Exercise 50

Identify the mistakes.

```
A:BARRY.LET          PAGE 1  LINE 23  COL 17      INSERT ON
L----!----!----!----!----!----!----!----!----!----!----!-----R
Omit Page number instruction ←
Ref LD/BY ←
←
Date as postmark ←
←
Dear Sirs ←
←
LAST AND FINAL DEMAND ←
←
Your account with us is now long overdue.  Our terms are 60
days nett; already 90 days have elapsed.  We have telephoned
on several occasions and sent statements with no satisfactory
conclusion. ←
←
▲▲We think we have been patient with you, but we
are unable to offer you extended credit facilities.  Therefore
we ask you to make payment in full to be received by ourselves
no later than *.  otherwise we shall be forced to take further
steps to recover the money through the County Court. ←
←
Yours faithfully ■
```

Original

OMIT PAGE NO.   USE BLOCK STYLE.
DATE AS POSTMARK.   REF LD/BY

Dear Sirs
LAST & FINAL DEMAND
Your a/c w us is now long overdue. Our terms are 60 days nett; already 90 days have elapsed.
run on (We have telephoned on several occasions & sent statements with no satisfactory conclusion. / We think we hv bn patient w y, but we, ~~as a small concern~~, are unable to offer you extended credit facilities. Therefore we ask y to make payment in full, to be received by ourselves no later than *, otherwise we shall be forced to take further steps to recover the money through the County Court. Yrs ffy
(obtain address off file as + when needed to put at bottom of letter).

Key to questions and exercises

1

End-of-section questions
1. Facsimile reproduction, colour
2. Draft, checked
3. Final version
4. Hardcopy, printout
5. Proof
6. Proofreader
7. House rules, house style

2

End-of-section questions
1. Word by word
2. Immediately
3. Margin, outwards
4. Draft, original
5. Draft, pen
6. Bottom

3

End-of-section questions
1. Original, detectable
2. *(a)* transposed letter   *(b)* adjacent key   *(c)* finger, hand   *(d)* double   *(e)* space
3. *(a)* spelling   *(b)* nouns, verbs   *(c)* homophone   *(d)* punctuation   *(e)* hyphenation   *(f)* capitalisation
4. *(a)* opposite   *(b)* sense   *(c)* appear   *(d)* nonsense
5. Repeated, omitted
6. *(a)* pattern   *(b)* impossible   *(c)* checked

4

End-of-section questions
1. Information lines, cursor
2. Indenting, symbols
3. Paragraph, word wraparound, reform
4. Sentence, last
5. Gaps, justification, end
6. Moves over, right-hand margin
7. Cleared (or cancelled)

5

End-of-section questions
1. Leave unchanged
2. Insert in the text the matter which is indicated in the margin
3. Delete (remove the unwanted item)
4. Delete and close up
5. Change capital letters to lower case letters
6. Change the lower case letters to capital letters
7. Centre the matter which is between the markers
8. Transpose the characters or words
9. Insert space between the lines or paragraphs
10. Insert a space between words

6

Exercises
1. (a) thand, litter   (b) wither: colon instead of semi-colon
2. Benefitted, consummable
3. 'computor' for 'computer'
4. Words omitted: promoted, never; comma needed after 'Timbuctoo'; 'secretary' should have lower case 's'
5. beleive, Shiela, Einstien, recieve, biege, seive
6. Word omitted: only; hyphen inserted; 'in to' for 'into'
7. Word omitted: and
8. Line of text between 'within' and 'within' is missing
9. Line of text between 'is' and 'is' is missing
10. Lines 1 and 2 – 'with' repeated
    Lines 5 and 6 – 'cur' repeated
    Line 7 – 'labelled' incomplete
11. Line 3 – '75' should be '76'
    Line 5 – 1 April does not follow 14 March
    Line 5 – 31 April is an impossible date
12. The sum should read: 2869 +
                           7011
                           9880
13. Minster is a building – word should be Minister. The Roman numerals should read I Corinthians Chapter XIII verse xiii
14. Line 4 – figures 021 transposed
    Line 5 – 031 should be 021
15. Line 1 – comma and quotation marks omitted
    Line 2 – quotation marks omitted
16. (a) Line 1 – quotation marks omitted
       Line 2 – quotation marks in wrong place
       Line 3 – comma inserted after 'form'
       Line 4 – comma omitted after 'below'
    (b) Line 5 – full-stop omitted after 'don't'
       Line 6 – initial capital required for 'Now'; full-stop inserted after 'switch', initial capital inserted ('From')
17. (a) Line 3 – 'of' instead of 'or'
    (b) Line 2 – 'or' instead of 'of'
    (c) Line 1 – open punctuation used in draft
       Line 2 – lower case r for 'Reassessment'
              lower case e for 'Effect'
              'on' instead of 'of'
       Line 3 – lower case f for 'Family'
              lower case s for 'Schooling'
              full stop omitted after 'America'
    (d) Line 1 – 'expensive' instead of 'extensive'

	(e) Line 4 – 'of' instead of 'or'
18	Lines 4/5 – 'inpacked' instead of 'impact'
19	Line 3 – 'red' instead of 'read'
	Line 6 – 'dilated' instead of 'deleted'
	Line 9 – 'annually' instead of 'only'; 'dating' instead of 'editing'
20	*(a)* Line 3 – 'who's' instead of 'whose'
	(b) Line 1 – 'advise' instead of 'advice'
	Line 2 – 'independant' instead of 'independent'
	(c) Line 2 – 'loose' instead of 'lose'
	Line 3 – 'practice' instead of 'practise'
21	Line 1 – lower case letters instead of initial capitals for 'Post Office'
	Line 2 – initial capital for 'mailing'
22	*(a)* Line 2 – 'has' should read 'have'
	(b) Line 4 – 'are' should read 'am'
23	Line 1 – too many spaces between 'The' and 'telephone'
	Line 2 – too many spaces between 'require' and 'is'
	Line 3 – too many spaces between '01' and '234'
24	Each 'time' is rendered in a different style
25	*(a)* Line 2 – omission of hyphen in 're-establish'
	Line 4 – omission of hyphen in 'co-operation'
	(b) Line 3 – omission of hyphen in 'pre-emption'
	Line 4 – insertion of hyphen in 'prerogative'
26	Line 1 – wrong division of 'Physiotherapist' creates a sound change ('Physiothe' and 'rapist')
	Line 3 – wrong division of 'Police' creates a sound change
	Line 4 – wrong division of 'Fathers' creates a sound change
27	The sentence should read: An Agreement has been reached between L Lumsden and O Cochrane
28	*(a)* Line 1 – 'if' instead of 'for'
	Line 2 – Full-stop after abbreviation 'recd.' has been interpreted as a punctuation mark and an initial capital has been inserted in the next word
	Line 2 – The abbreviation for 'this morning', ie 'am.' has been interpreted as the whole word 'am'
	Line 4 – The abbreviation for 'you' ('y') has been interpreted as 'your'
	Line 5 – The word 'early' has been interpreted as the two words 'ear by'
	There should be no punctuation mark in the middle of the 24-hour clock time
	(b) Line 3 – The shorthand for 'able to' has been interpreted as 'about'
29	*Postcard.* Line 5 – Date uses a combination of Roman and Arabic numbers. The date should always be in Arabic.
	Line 6 – 'interveiw' instead of 'interview'
	Line 7 – Roman numeral I used instead of Arabic 1 in the date and time. (Ambiguities arise. Is this intended to be 2nd February or 11th November?)
	Decimal point in the middle of 24-hour clock time
	Line 8 – 'conveneint' instead of 'convenient'
	Line 10 – 'an' repeated; 'apointment' instead of 'appointment'
	Reverse – Confidential information should never be mailed openly on a postcard. A separate envelope marked 'CONFIDENTIAL' should be provided so that the postcard can be sealed.
	Line 2 – Cannot be 'Mrs' and 'Esq'
	Line 3 – 'Il0 (Roman and Arabic mixed); Shaw Crescent
	Line 4 – 'Town' should be typed in capitals
	Line 5 – 'Lancs' instead of 'Lincs'
30	2 2 2 1 2 1 3 3 2
31	The notices should read:

FOR SALE: FRESHLY-CAUGHT-CRAB SANDWICHES

FOR SALE: TABLE WITH QUEEN-ANNE-STYLE BOW LEGS

ELECTRIC TYPEWRITER WITH GOLF-BALL HEAD FOR SALE

I bought a fresh salmon for your birthday, but I'm afraid it flavoured everything in the fridge.

NOTICE IN A GREENGROCER'S SHOP: Owing to the drought, leeks are scarce this month.

The Golconda diamond is 47.29 carats and has been certified as flawless.

These pills are dangerous and should be locked in a cupboard.
Keep them away from children.

It is inadvisable to exceed the stated dose.
(An alternative may be: It is not advisable to exceed the stated dose.)

32   Column 129 is unlikely to precede column 127. Check both. (If both are correct, the lower column may have to be moved up.)
Line 2 – A whole line has been omitted
Line 4 – Semicolon has been inserted instead of a colon after 'FOUND'
       'bugie' instead of 'budgie'
       space omitted between 'a lot'
Line 6 – quotation marks omitted
Line 7 – 'CAR' instead of 'CAT'
Line 8 – 'Vinder' instead of 'Finder'
Line 9 – 'Laddies' instead of 'Ladies'
Line 10 – 'bxo' instead of 'box'
Line 12 – 'dot' instead of 'dog'
Line 13 – 'dash-hound' instead of 'dachshund'
Line 15 – hyphen omitted between column number and WANTED
Line 16 – lower case p instead of capitals for 'Piano'
Line 17 – 'tuna' instead of 'tune'
Line 19 – lower case m for 'Manager'
Line 20 – 'separated' should have a comma after it, not a hyphen
       'tail' instead of 'tall'

33   The notices should read:

FIRE NOTICE   Do not obstruct the fire doors.

NOTICE   To raise the alarm, break the glass when fire occurs.

SAFETY NOTICE   Keep the gangways clear

STAFF NOTICE   A door key has been found. Please contact Office Manager.

WARNING   Please mind your head when leaving your seat

Holiday Rota   Please notify Personnel Officer of holiday requirements by 2 June

34   (a) Line 4 – 'chairman' for 'Chairman'
       Line 5 – hyphen inserted in 'shareholders'
       Line 6 – 'proffit' instead of 'profit'
    (b) Line 1 – 'Cockrayne' instead of 'Cochayne'
       Line 2/3 – 'Richard I' needs to be kept together so that 'I' is not read as
           a pronoun.
       Line 4 – 'Stafford' instead of 'Stratford'
    (c) Line 1 – 32 July is an impossible date
       Line 5 – '10%' instead of '16%'
       Line 6 – 50% instead of '5%'
    (d) Line 8 – 'restraining' instead of 'retraining'

35   Line 1 – 'Wyatt' instead of 'Myatt'
Line 2 – '80' instead of '18', 'Grenville Row instead of Glenville Road'
Line 3 – 'SUTTAM COALFEEL' instead of 'SUTTON COLDFIELD'
Line 4 – '58W' instead of '5HW'

36   Paragraph 3 – 'exceot' for 'except'
       right-hand bracket for left-hand bracket
       hyphen omitted, full-stop omitted

Paragraph 6 – Initial capitals required
Paragraph 10 – Insert '(No underscore required)'
Paragraph 11 – 'dictionery' for 'dictionary' (twice); 'ckecked' for 'checked'
Paragraph 12 – Paragraph numbers are transposed and read '21'
Paragraph 13 – Hyphen omitted; sentence missing

37 Main heading and shoulder headings in lower case
Arguments Against   Paragraph 2 – 'needs' omitted; 'ban' for 'can'
'guaged' for 'gauged'
Paragraph 4 – 'extention' for 'extension'

38 *Memo*   date omitted
Line 4 – underscore instead of colon after 'entry'
Verse 1 – Line 5 – hyphen used instead of semicolon
Verse 2 – Line 5 – 'Tgat' instead of 'That'
'plots' has been left in, when author had changed the text to 'words'

39 Letter undated
Lines 1 and 6 – 'Thompoon' instead of 'Thompson' (twice)
Line 9 – apostrophe omitted
Line 12 – decimal point missing, 'singed' instead of 'signed'
Line 13 – full stop instead of comma

40 Letter undated
Addressee: 'Tom Askew' for 'Thomas Kew'
'20 Twostone Road' for '22 Stone Road'
'LESTER' for 'LEICESTER'
'SJU' for '5JU'
Body: Line 1 – full stop for comma after 'letter', comma for full stop after 'morning',
initial capital for 'received', lower case 'w' for 'We'
Lines 3 and 4 – Overlapping sentences
Omit s from 3rd line of heading

41 *Suggested text:*

On arrival, holiday-makers must stop at the office and register. They will be given a numbered plot, and a sticker (or 'a sticky badge') for their car.

The office will be open from 0900 hours to 1300 hours for payment of camping fees but reception will be open from 0700 hours to 2300 hours.

TARIFF
Each adult
Each child under 5 years
plugs

42 No commands inserted to remove the default, so letter will be numbered page 1 when printed out.

Screen symbols in comment line indicate that a hard carriage return was used at the end of every line, thus word wraparound was not used. If new information is added the text will only partially reform.

The name of the company where Mr French works has been omitted from the addressee portion of the letter.
Lines 11 and 12 – 'for' has been repeated

43 All the proof correction symbols have been incorporated accurately; no page numbers

44 The spaces between the ellipsis dots have not been protected, so the second dot has moved on to the next line and the computer is querying it.

Justified right-hand margin has caused some wide gaps between words to be created by soft spaces. The work may be easier to read with a ragged right margin.

45 Forgotten commands. The operator has forgotten to centre the heading and underline it. (Carriage return symbols and status line information indicate that the operator has moved on.)

46 Paragraph not reformed when new information was inserted. No hard spaces after the word 'long'.

47	Quotation marks omitted after 'Vendors'. Lower case p for 'purchaser'. Consistency required. Either both Vendor and Purchaser have initial capitals or both have lower case letters. Right hand brackets omitted twice.
48	No obvious commands to remove automatic page numbering
	Memo not dated for tomorrow as required
	Keyboarding mistakes: 'cconomy' for 'economy', 'stationary' for 'stationery', hyphen omitted in 'co-operation'. Two hard spaces missing after punctuation mark. 'would' instead of 'should', 'e' repeated in middle of 'wherever'
49	Toggle action command not cleared after 'as soon as possible'; therefore the remainder of the tear-off slip will be underlined.
	Tabulator stops have been set for two columns and were used appropriately until the leader dots after 'Signed', then hard spaces were used, and the date is not aligned with the right-hand column of leader dots.
	Lower case 'd' for 'Department'
50	Paragraph 1/2 – When the paragraph was divided, the two hard spaces were moved to the beginning of the next paragraph and have not been removed.
	Paragraph 2 – Space at the end of the line indicates that information has been deleted, but the paragraph has not been reformed. Comma missing after 'full'. Full stop instead of comma after variable insert point (the space where the date is to appear)

External examination questions

Academic

1. In a centralised word processing section, the Supervisor is vital to the efficiency of both the system and operators.

    Describe: (a) the role and duties of the Word Processing Supervisor; and
    (b) the qualities such a person should possess.

    LCCI IP (1983)

2. Select 5 of the following items and show that you clearly understand the difference between:
    (a) Merging text and joining text
    (b) Cut and paste and block exchange
    (c) Reformatting and reforming
    (d) A widow line and an orphan line
    (e) Screenreading and proofreading
    (f) A justified right-hand margin and a ragged right-hand margin.

    LCCI IP (Higher Stage) (1984)

3. (a) Name and explain the types of errors which an operator would be expected to identify when proofreading hard copy.
    Give one example of each item which you explain.
    (b) Briefly explain the skills, other than proofreading, which are required of an operator.

    LCCI IP (Higher Stage) (1984)

4. Explain briefly what is meant by 4 of the following terms:
    (a) Off-line printing   (d) Cursor
    (b) Shared logic   (e) Boilerplating
    (c) Wraparound   (f) CPU

    LCCI WP (1983)

5. Explain what is meant by 4 of the following terms:
    (a) Workstation   (d) Text editing
    (b) Status lines   (e) VDU
    (c) Variables   (f) Teletext

    LCCI WP (1984)

Practical

1 Mr Jones' wife has prepared the following rough draft of the route for Mr Khamil to take to his hotel from the Mather factory.

   Mr Jones wishes you to retype it for him. Proof read the directions, circling any errors you find, so that you know to correct them when you retype. You can assume that the directions are factually correct.

   Leave the building by the main gate, truning left into Ferngate Hill. After approximately 100 yards, turn right into Lowville Road (this will take you under a small Bridge). Continue along Lowville Road to the second set of traffic lights. Turn right at these lights and you will now be in a one-way system until the road divided.   take the right fork and almost immediatly take a sharp right turn (this will be signposted multi_story car park). At the top of the slope you will find the George Hotel car park alongside the multi-storey car park. A single suit of rooms has been booked for Mr Khamil at the George.

   RSA WP Stage I (1983)

2 One of the managers for whom you work 'phones to enquire whether the addition to his report is ready for collection. You find that it has been typed but not printed. You know that the girl who typed it was feeling unwell yesterday, so you decide to check the work before it is despatched. The report is required for a meeting later that morning. It was transcribed from audio dictation.

   Please circle the errors which you would correct.

   The knew building has been designed to accomodate the entire Pharmaceutical Developement Departmnt. It is envisaged that building will commence on 15 Febuary next year and will be completed in approximately one year's time.

   The existing car parking facilities will be affected due to the presence of contractors' vehicles. It is therefore suggested that the area previously reserved fro visitors be make available to employees from the above date. The attatched sketch indicates the proposed plans.

   RSA WP Stage I (1983)

3 The supervisor asks you to proof read everything which Julie types for the first week. Although generally Julie is fairly accurate, her spelling, punctuation and grammar need carefully checking.

   Circle each error she has made in the following passage.

   Graduate recruitment will continue during 1983 at a level similar to 1982– ie two graduates will be recruited each months

   They will undertake a structured trainig programme ensureing that in there first-year with the company they gain experience of the Computer, Manufacturing, research and Technical Divisions. And they will also be seconded for a period on the shopfloor.

During their second year with the company, graduates will specialise in selected departments and will them be offered a choice of permanence employment within that department or a third year gaining further experience in another department.

RSA WP Stage I (1983)

4. The office junior, who has recently attended a word processing training course, has been helping you to type a technical report. This is the first time she has used the office equipment and her work needs careful checking.

   Circle each error she has made in the following passage.

Great care must be exercised in ensuring the validity of data. If there is going to be only one source for this data then it's validitity canot be tested against other data files. With a database, if the data is wrong then every application using that data will be wrong. this problem is increasingly recognised. In buisness activities an error in the database may result in incorrect invioces. Were the data is con-concerned with records about people, an error in the database can be fare more singificant. An example of this is where incorrect data has beeen stored in a database concerned with credit ratings.

RSA WP Stage I (1984)

RSA Teacher's Diploma in Typewriting

This is a task from RSA Part 1: Theory and application of typewriting (1983), reproduced here for study and discussion.

TASK (i)

Variations in pitch and typeface do not matter in this task. You will have to squeeze or spread characters. Alignment is important, ie your insertions, even though they may be of different size and shape, should be level (at the bottom of letters) with adjacent characters on the typing line. Also, wherever possible, avoid the overtyping effect of characters too close to each other.

You receive the following note from your Supervisor, together with page one of the second draft of Report 12890. You will need to check this against the corrected first draft.

(Drafts on the following pages)

> Typist: Stella is away, + she had started the second draft of Report 12890. She had even started correcting p1 (her typewriter broke down!) Will you finish/correcting this first page of the 2nd draft please. I particularly do not want it re-typed, but I don't think she has corrected all the mistakes which were in the first draft (some spellings look wrong to me!) — nor all of her own in the second draft. Check them against each other, + just let me have an accurate sheet for the author. For this purpose mixed typefaces do not matter, just so long as the right words + letters are there.
>
> JB

Corrected first draft (page 1)

```
REPORT 12890
```

It is no~~t~~ (now) possible to revise the off~~e~~(e)r which is the content of
Contract A/428/V(small v.), and/(the) terms of reference of this ~~r~~(R)eport concern
th~~is~~(e) revision in ~~view~~ (the light) of re~~c~~(c)ent and current trends within (the)
industry.

Sources of information are available in the organi~~z~~(s)ation and
~~were~~ (are) supplemented by published ~~details~~ (data). Th~~is~~(e) ~~d~~(D)epartment liased (check spelling)
w~~ith~~(with) other departments within the organisation, and with other
organisations, on the construction of graphs and tables, (& for effective diagrammatical presentation) of
~~st~~ (previously unpublished) statistic~~al information for printing present~~.

Many companies have ~~designed~~ (developed) their products to accom-
modate features ~~prividing~~ (which provide) fascilities for requirements t~~ha~~(wh)t have accompanied the growth in technology. In order to ensure we maintain our progress
in the (is) field it is imp~~o~~(necy)rtant for us to embark on an
extensive programme of research. To this end it
is proposed to finance the work of a research team
through the medium of a two-year project to be designed
and undertaken by an organisation who will recriut (? spelling) and
direct it's own employees in work designed to lead to
the solution of the problems and needs to be outlined
by the Dept (Type both in full) (see App.1). This/(work) will be/(the) subject of Tender
to be announced by newspaper advert (Type in full) for response by (the) end of

Second draft (page 1)

REPORT 12890

It is now possible to revise the offer which is t e content of
 ontract A/428/v, and the terms of reference of this Report concern
this revision in the light of recent and current trends within the
industry. Sources of information are available in the organisation
and were supplemented by published data. Yhe Department liaised
with other departments within the organisation, and with other
organisations, on the constructing of graphs and tables, and for
effective diagrammatical presentation of previously unpublished stati-
istics.
Many companies have developed hteir products to accomodate
features which provide fascilities for requirements which
have accompanied-the growth in technology. In order to
ensure we maintain our progress in this field it is
necessary for us to embark on an extendive programme of
research. To this end it is proposed to finance the work
of a research team through the medium of a two-year
project to be designed and undertaken by an organisation
who will recruit and direct its own employees in work
desinged to lead to the solution of the problems and needs
to be outlind by the Departmnnt (see Appendix 1). This
work will by the subject of Tender to be announced by
newspaper advertisment for response by the end of

Index

adjacent letter (error)	12	handwriting	32-4
agreement of nouns/verbs	27	hard carriage return	40, 58
audiotranscription	26, 27, 81, 90	hardcopy	5, 47
		hard spaces	41, 42, 58
automatic page numbering	49, 57	homophones	6, 28-30
		hot zone	38, 58
brackets	6	house rules and styles	6
British Standards Institution	60	hyphenation	6, 31
capitalisation	6, 28	"impossible" figures	19, 22
comment line	57	incorrect display (VDU)	42, 51, 52
compound words	6	incremental printer	58
context	5	indented style	6
control flags	39, 40, 57	input mode	58
cursor	36, 57	inserted words	6
dates	23	insertion errors (VDU)	45, 46, 54
dedicated word processor	57, 59	justified left margin	58
default	38, 49, 51, 57	justified right margin	43, 44, 46, 50, 58
deletion errors	45, 46, 47, 54	keyboarding errors	6, 12-13, 18-19
dictating (for checking)	11		
disk drive	36	layout	6
division of words	6, 31	line(s) omitted	16-17
draft	3, 5	line spacing	6
edit mode	37, 45, 54, 57, 58	marginal correction symbols	9
		misinterpretation errors	53
editing feature	53	mistranscription, audio	26, 27
ellipsis	43, 44	shorthand	34, 35, 75
errors, types of	6, 12-35		
searching for	8	near-homophones	29-30
facsimile	5	omitted words	6, 15, 16
faircopy	5, 6	letter	12
figures, "impossible"	19, 22	line	16, 17
alignment	21	punctuation	24
consistency of style	20, 21	space	12
easily checkable	19	open punctuation	6
Roman numerals	20	original	3, 5, 6
final version	5	orphan line	56, 58
forgotten commands	49, 51		
fractions	6	page breaks	56
fully blocked style	6	photocopy	5, 6
grammatical errors	6, 27	postcodes	22

printout	5, 36, 41, 50, 54	sophisticated software	59
proof	5	spacing after punctuation	6, 30
proof correction symbols	8-10, 60-3	extra	30
proofreader	5	omitted	12, 30
proofreading (definition)	3	with figures	31
protected spaces	43, 44, 58	spelling errors	6, 13-15
punctuation, open	6	inconsistent	14
omitted	24	standalone	57, 59
on VDU	41	status (formatting) line	36, 59
"pairs"	23	substitution of word	25, 26
		symbols	6
quotation marks	6	marginal correction	9, 10
		proof correction	8-10, 60-3
ragged margin	39, 43, 44, 49, 58	temporary (coded) margin	51, 52
reforming	40, 44-7, 52, 58	text movement error	53
		toggle	59
repetition of words	17, 18	action commands	48
of syllable	18	transposed characters	6, 12
reverse tone	52, 59	types of error	6, 12-35
Roman numerals	20, 21	typographic errors	6, 12, 13
ruler line	37, 59	unjustified margin	39
screenreading	36-59	VDU (visual display unit)	5, 36, 59
screen symbols	39, 40, 51, 52, 57	widow line	56, 59
		word string	44, 59
scrolling	59	left out	15-18
semi-blocked style	6	repeated	17-18
shorthand	34, 35	substitution	25-6
signs, proof correction	8-10, 60-3	wraparound	39, 40, 51, 52, 58, 59
soft carriage return	59	working in pairs (for checking)	11
softcopy	5, 39, 41, 59	wrong command	55
soft spaces	43, 44		
software	59		